CITY BIRDS
Country Birds

How Anyone Can Attract Birds to Their Feeder

by Sharon Stiteler, The BirdChick

Adventure Publications, Inc.
Cambridge, Minnesota

To my Mom, a lady who supported my interest in birds, fostered a love of reading and taught me the value of a good fart joke.

Special Thanks

Melissa Block, Val Cunningham, Steve Endres, Ron Gauthier, Neil Gaiman, Lorraine Garland, Terri Graves, Carrol Henderson, Tony Hertzel, Bob Janssen, Mom, Lori Lundeen, Dennis Martin, Ian and Margery Punnett, Gordon Slabaugh, Dr. and Mrs. Paul Strange, Stan Tekiela and my poor husband.

And a most important thanks to all the people I have met over the years who feed birds and who taught me so much with their wonderful stories about their yards. Bird specialty store employees would not be nearly as smart as they are without customers telling them about their yard happenings.

Cover and book design by Jonathan Norberg

Photo credits by photographer and page number:

Cover photo by Stan Tekiela
Joel Bahma: 155 (top) **Birds Choice:** 62, 65 (top) **Amber Burnette:** 90 (bottom), 107 (right), 148 **Karen S. Cramer:** 20 (top) **Geoff Dennis:** 47 **Droll Yankees:** 73, 74 **Monica Leachman:** 177 **Maslowski Productions:** 104 (both) **Mike McDowell:** 83, 124 (top) **Susan Merchant:** 72 (top right) **Elizabeth M. Ostwald:** 71 (top right) **Bill Schmoker:** 14, 17, 36 (left), 39 (both), 79 (top, bottom left), 80 (bottom), 86, 93 (bottom), 95 (top), 96 (bottom right), 110 (top), 136 (middle), 140 (top), 160, 172, 176 **Shutterstock:** 10, 29, 30 (top), 31, 36 (right), 76, 154 (top), 167 (bottom), 173, 174 **Sharon M. S. Snyder:** 20 (bottom), 102 (top), 106 (bottom) **Nonda Surratt:** 128 (bottom middle), 135, 136 (top), 139, 141 **Swarovski Optik N. A. Ltd.:** 186 (right) **Stan Tekiela:** 22, 24, 28 (both), 53 (bottom), 55, 58 (right), 59, 60, 64 (top), 65 (bottom), 66 (top), 68 (bottom), 71 (bottom), 72 (top left), 78, 79 (bottom right), 80 (top), 84, 89, 92 (bottom), 93 (top right), 94 (middle), 96 (bottom left), 97 (all), 98 (bottom), 99, 100 (both), 108, 110 (bottom), 111 (bottom), 112 (top), 113 (all), 115 (top), 116 (top), 119, 120 (both), 121, 122 (top), 123, 124 (bottom), 125, 126, 128 (top, bottom right and left), 129 (top), 132 (top), 133, 136 (bottom), 137 (both), 140 (bottom), 142, 147 (bottom), 150, 152 (both), 153 (bottom), 155 (bottom three), 156 (both), 157, 161, 164, 166, 167 (top), 169, 187 **Wild Birds Unlimited, Inc.:** 26, 32, 34 (bottom right), 40 (both), 41, 67 (top), 70, 81, 95 (bottom), 165 **Wild Birds Unlimited, Inc./James R. Carpenter:** 42, 69 (left), 111 (middle), 129 (middle) **Tammy Wolfe:** 11, 72 (bottom right), 87 (bottom), 88 (top), 112 (bottom), 115 (bottom), 117 (top) **Julie Zickefoose:** 38 **Jim Zipp:** 12, 21, 53 (middle), 58 (left), 63 (top), 66 (bottom), 93 (top left), 117 (bottom), 118, 129 (bottom), 145, 158, 180 **Sharon Stiteler:** all other photos

9-23-08   598.072
          STi   OCLC
                 gift

10 9 8 7 6 5 4 3 2 1

Table of Contents

Setting the Table

CHAPTER TEN 151
Surprise Guests

CHAPTER ELEVEN 159
Common Questions

CHAPTER TWELVE   171
Case Studies

CHAPTER THIRTEEN   181
Beyond Bird Feeding
(I've discovered I'm a bird nut. Now what?)

RESOURCES   189

INDEX   190

ABOUT THE AUTHOR   192

Intro

You're probably opening this book and thinking, "Yeah, right, I can get birds coming to my yard. No way, chickie, I live in an apartment/town-home/condo, and the only feathered friends in my neighborhood are pigeons, a.k.a. flying rats. Don't come to me with your song and dance of how anyone can attract wild birds. I won't believe your lies, I tell you!"

Okay, so maybe it's not that dramatic in your head, but lean in close now and read carefully. Whether you live in a condo with views of skyscrapers, the third floor of an apartment building or a busy suburb, you can get some really nifty birds coming to your windows!

Birds are everywhere, yet many people tend to overlook birds that have adapted to humans quite well and will gladly visit food, water or shelter that you might put out for them. I'm not just talking blackbirds and pigeons here; I am talking about bona fide cool birds: Northern Cardinals, House Finches, Baltimore Orioles, Black-capped Chickadees and, dare I say it (yes, I dare), hawks! Yes, my friend, birds that were once perceived as visible only way out in the country or on Animal Planet can be as close as your bedroom window.

In rare cases bird feeding can get out of control. Not long ago, a small neighborhood in Monticello, Minnesota, started feeding a small flock of Trumpeter Swans that wintered on the Mississippi River. (A nearby power plant keeps the water from freezing.) Now, over a thousand swans can be found feeding in the neighborhood, along with Canada Geese, Mallards and other waterfowl. The birds go through over 1,200 pounds of corn a day!

Bird feeding has long been thought of as something that only a grand-parent does, but feeding birds shouldn't be limited to the over-sixty crowd. Anyone can do it (and enjoy it) and can put as much time and energy into it as they want.

This book is designed to help you get started. If you decide you'd like to feed birds, you don't have to go hog wild and have fourteen bird feeders hanging off your balcony. Go slow and pace yourself because, as you will learn with this book, not only is it important to put feeders out to attract birds, it's also important to place them correctly, fill them with good stuff and keep them clean. Starting slow and simple will keep you from buying the wrong feeder for your home.

Tufted Titmice are friendly little birds that will come quite close to humans when feeding.

Though it's true that you can get really great birds in the city, habitat is still a factor. Some birds, such as House Finches, will show up no matter what. Others, such as woodpeckers, will be more inclined to show up in neighborhoods with lots of trees. Included in this book are tips and tricks to overcome limitations that are inherent to living in non-rural areas.

These are guidelines based not only on my personal experience, but also on stories shared with me from customers and birding friends over the years. If there is one thing I have learned working in a bird feed store, it's that no two pieces of prop-erty are alike. What works in one person's backyard doesn't always work in everyone's yard. So I've included lots of options, strategies and Plan Bs to help you figure out what works best for the place where you live.

Some people find experimentation very helpful, so don't be afraid to try that with your feeders. Playing around is a great way to find what works best for the birds in your yard.

Again, this book is a guideline filled with some good advice. If the birds don't always do what I say in the book, it's not you; it's them. They just haven't read the book yet to find out what they are supposed to be doing.

If they aren't doing what's listed in this book, feel free to leave a copy for them outside so they will learn what to do. Keep in mind that this trick only works with birds that you have trained to read.

Sometimes birds don't follow the book. This Rose-breasted Grosbeak apparently doesn't know that it's not supposed to visit suet feeders!

CHAPTER ONE

Getting Started: Assess Your Bird Feeding Situation

Attracting birds can be as simple or complicated as you like. To get a handle on your property's potential, take a look at your yard and ask some questions.

OPPOSITE: Baltimore Oriole

Where Do You Live?

The first step is determining what kind of housing you are living in. Easy! The type of housing can impact whether you're allowed to feed birds, the types of feeders you choose and where you can place them for the best effect.

If you are in a house you have the most options. You get to decide if you want to feed birds and whether to mount your bird feeders in trees (assuming you have some), on poles in your yard or brackets on your deck.

Apartment dwellers have different concerns. The first is to find out whether or not feeding or attracting birds is allowed. If you can, find this out before you move in. If there is nothing specific in your lease agreement, don't assume that you have the green light to feed birds. It's always best to get answers up front from managers or property owners.

Another concern for apartment dwellers is how many stories off the ground can you be and still attract birds? A good rule of thumb is to look where you are in relation to trees. If you are at the tops of the trees or lower you have an excellent chance of attracting birds. If you look down at the tops of trees from several stories, then your best (maybe only) option would be looking into getting some sort of nest platform for cliff-dwelling species (such as Peregrine Falcons) installed on your balcony (not very easy to do unless you have an "in" with U.S. Fish and Wildlife).

If you live in a town-house or condo you might have more options, but don't assume that you are allowed to feed. Many associations don't allow feeding or only allow bird feeding in specific areas. Also, some associations only allow certain items or a

Place your feeders where they are easy to see.

set number of items on decks. I know whereof I speak. My mother lives in a condo and has become her block's warden. We joke and call her Deputy Fife, but if you have the wrong items on your deck, boy howdy, you'd bet-ter believe she will leave you a note. Find out what the rules are before you bring out the feeders.

Where Do the Birds Live?

	Heavily Wooded	Mildly Wooded	Few to No Trees	Marsh/wetland
MOST LIKELY ◉				
KINDA' LIKELY ◉				
HIGHLY UNLIKELY ○				
Blackbird, Red-winged	◉	◉	◉	◉
Bluebird, Eastern	○	◉	◉	◉
Bunting, Indigo	◉	◉	◉	◉
Cardinal, Northern	◉	◉	◉	◉
Catbird, Gray	◉	◉	◉	◉
chickadees	◉	◉	◉	◉
Crow, American	◉	◉	◉	◉
Dove, Mourning	○	◉	◉	◉
Finch, House	◉	◉	◉	◉
Goldfinch, American	◉	◉	◉	◉
Goose, Canada	○	◉	◉	◉
Grackle, Common	◉	◉	◉	◉
Grosbeak, Rose-breasted	◉	◉	◉	○
Hawk, Broad-winged	◉	◉	◉	◉
Hawk, Cooper's	◉	◉	◉	◉
Hawk, Red-tailed	◉	◉	◉	◉
Hawk, Sharp-shinned	◉	◉	◉	◉
Hummingbird, Ruby-throated	◉	◉	◉	◉
Jay, Blue	◉	◉	◉	◉
Junco, Dark-eyed	◉	◉	◉	◉
Kestrel, American	○	◉	◉	◉
Killdeer	○	◉	◉	◉
Mallard	○	◉	◉	◉
Martin, Purple	○	◉	◉	◉
Mockingbird, Northern	○	◉	◉	◉
nuthatches	◉	◉	◉	○
orioles	◉	◉	◉	◉
Pheasant, Ring-necked	◉	◉	◉	◉
Pigeon, Rock	○	◉	◉	◉
Redpoll, Common	◉	◉	◉	◉
Robin, American	◉	◉	◉	◉
Sparrow, Chipping	○	◉	◉	◉
Sparrow, House	◉	◉	◉	◉
Sparrow, Song	◉	◉	◉	◉
Sparrow, White-throated	◉	◉	◉	◉
Starling, European	◉	◉	◉	◉
Swallow, Tree	○	◉	◉	◉
Thrasher, Brown	○	◉	◉	◉
Titmouse, Tufted	◉	◉	◉	○
towhees	◉	◉	◉	○
Turkey, Wild	◉	◉	◉	◉
woodpeckers	◉	◉	◉	◉
Wren, Carolina	◉	◉	◉	○
Wren, House	◉	◉	◉	◉

Habitat

Another factor to consider as you assess your bird feeding situation is habitat. Look around and see what features are nearby, and what features are right in your yard or complex. The habitat determines the types of birds you can attract. If there is any kind of water close by, you have a big bonus in attracting birds. You can always find great birds next to lakes, creeks, ponds, rivers, marshes and wetlands. Birds need water for moisture and many birds eat insects that breed on or near water. If you don't have it, don't freak out, I'll show you simple ways of adding water to your yard.

Wooded Suburban Yard

» **Pros:** The older your neighborhood, the better, because this usually means mature trees. If you have lots of trees, birds can use them for several purposes. First is food; some trees produce seeds and fruit that we may never notice or begin to find appetizing, but birds see them as an immense grocery store. Trees can serve as shelter for roosting at night or in winter and they may also function as a great place for some birds to build nests.

If you have a heavily wooded yard, keep feeders a good ten feet away from trees.

» **Cons:** If you have trees, you will have squirrels. No amount of trapping and removing or even nuclear bombing will get them out of your yard. Something to remember is that squirrels can jump five feet vertically from a standing position on the ground. They can also jump ten feet horizontally from any perch including deck rails, lawn furniture and trees.

» **Strategies:** Look around and see if you have an open spot where you could put a feeder on a pole with a squirrel blocker or baffle. If you do not have an open spot that is ten feet from all launching objects you may have to consider a squirrel-resistant feeder.

New Development

» **Pros:** The newness of the development will determine the amount of birds you have. Land with lots of trees attracts different birds than open fields. Open areas can attract a nice variety of birds including goldfinches, robins, swallows and Eastern Bluebirds.

» **Cons:** Immediately after the habitat has changed it may take a while to attract birds, especially if the area was heavily wooded before the housing went up. If the lot was heavily wooded and all the trees were torn down, birds that prefer a wooded habitat had to move on. If there has been lots of construction going on, even birds that prefer open habitat will not stick around.

American Robins sometimes build their nests on new homes where trees have been recently removed.

» **Strategies:** It may take the neighborhood a year or two to calm down before you see significant bird activity. Keep your feeders clean and filled with good black-oil sunflower seed mixes, and offer water. The birds will return; you'll just need to be patient.

City Area

» **Pros:** This is an area that could be on a busy street with a downtown skyline outside your window. Take heart, even you can attract birds. People in buildings as high as six stories have an excellent chance of attracting a variety of birds, including House Finches, chickadees, nuthatches and cardinals, not just Rock Pigeons or crows.

» **Cons:** While you can attract some delightful birds, doing so can require more patience and creativity in heavily urban areas. Quite a few birds thrive in metro areas. Hey, if New York can have Red-tailed Hawks nesting on buildings, you should be able to get a chickadee visiting from time to time.

» **Strategies:** Even if you do not have a balcony you can still attract birds right up to your windows. There are several styles of feeders that suction-cup right on to glass. These small feeders are worth the effort. In some cases you can install plant brackets into your window frames and hang most feeders.

With a little patience and the right food, you can get great birds–including the colorful Northern Cardinal–to come right up to an apartment window.

Where will it be fun and easy to watch birds?

Birds do not need us to feed them. Studies have shown that even in the worst of weather birds use your feeder for only about 20% of their overall diet. Birds have enough sense to rely on a variety of feeding areas, the only reason to feed birds is because you enjoy watching them. If you have your feeders set up in a nice little corner in your yard, but you have to perch with your knees on the kitchen sink and crane your head far to the left to see the feeder with one eye, there's no point.

Look out all your windows and think where it is going to be easiest to enjoy birds. Some people like to have feeders right outside the kitchen window to watch when they do dishes or cook. Some enjoy feeders outside the dining room window for mealtime entertainment, or in the family room. Some think it's a good idea to have a feeder outside the bedroom window, but keep in mind that birds eat right at the crack of dawn, and during nesting season a young Blue Jay begging for food can be an annoying start to the day.

Special Concerns for Urban Birds

One of my favorite phone calls was from a customer who asked about getting House Finches out of her yard. I asked if there a was a problem, since usually people enjoy House Finches at the feeders, especially the bright pink males. She answered, "No, they aren't causing a problem with other birds, but there are so many of them that it is ruining the aesthetics of the yard. I have too many feeding and it unbalances the colors. I would like to have fewer House Finches to balance out the colors of the birds."

I must tell you right now that you cannot control the birds—believe me, I have tried, and it's not possible. Yes, there are seeds and feeders that will help control some species—especially some blackbirds that can take over a feeder—but in the long run birds tend to have more control over us than we them. Think I'm joking? Wait until you get your first oriole showing up at your feeder and you find that part of your morning routine is putting fresh globs of grape jelly in the feeder, or the pang of guilt you feel when a male cardinal is angrily chipping at an empty feeder. Then you'll know what I mean about who has the most control in the human/wild bird relationship.

There are some factors that can keep birds coming or keep them going away. Here are a few things you can do as you assess your bird feeding station and prep your yard or complex for our avian neighbors.

Large flocks of House Finches will frequently come to feeders. Many people find that the more aggressive House Finch will sometimes drive away House Sparrows.

What Can Keep Birds Away

Young birds learning to fly, or exhausted migrants like this male Indigo Bunting, are especially vulnerable to cat predation.

» **Cats.** Cats are not the only reason why bird populations are down; there are several factors—one of the largest being habitat destruction—but every little bit a person can do really does help birds in the long run. If you have a cat that you let out in your yard and it gets only one bird here and there, you may think that your cat isn't a problem. But if you multiply one cat getting one or two birds a week by all the other neighborhoods where there is one cat getting one or two birds a week, that adds up quickly. Cats that consistently stalk a feeder will keep birds away.

Birds are most vulnerable when they are coming back from migration and are exhausted or when young birds are leaving the nest and learning to fly. It is the natural instinct for a cat to hunt, but most house cats are well fed by their owners and are hunting out of play. This could arguably be a problem for natural predators such as hawks that could be losing a potential meal to cats. If you have a cat and you want to attract birds, the best thing is to keep the cat inside.

» **Yard Traffic.** Birds will get used to some activity. There are a number of raptors that nest right next to highways, or robins that build nests low in trees right over sidewalks. However, when putting out your feeders, you might want to choose a quieter part of your property, away from dog kennels, children's play areas or entry ways to your home.

Window feeding can be great entertainment for cats. Birds do get used to the feline activity on the other side of the window.

If you are in a building with no yard or deck but only windows, don't fret about birds not coming in to feed because of traffic. There are several styles of suction cup feeders that are meant to be mounted right onto the glass, or you can get plant hangers that mount onto wooden window frames and are able to hold most bird feeders. Birds will come up to windows and will get used to family activities.

Some people set up bird feeders next to windows as entertainment for their cats. Birds learn quickly that no matter how much pouncing the cat tries they are perfectly safe. Larger birds such as Northern Cardinals and even Pileated Woodpeckers are wary about coming close, but they will learn to trust window feeders over time.

It has always seemed to me that the smaller a bird is, the less afraid of humans it is. Try wearing a red shirt around a hummingbird: you'll feel like Sheena, Queen of the Jungle as they fly in toward the color to determine if there is any food to be had. I suppose it's a matter of time before some-one comes up with a hummingbird nectar feeder shirt.

Some noise and traffic that birds won't tolerate include major landscaping or construction. If you are adding a room to your home or retiling your roof, that is enough to make birds hesitant to come to a feeder. Birds, like people, do not like change. For a bird, different is usually bad because that can mean there is a change in the food supply or safety. Construction with all sorts of movement and noise will make it difficult for a bird to watch and listen for predators, so they will move on to a quieter yard.

A change in the yard habitat will cause a change of species birds to leave the area. In my neck of the woods, we had to have several large elm trees removed by the city because of Dutch Elm Disease. Many good roosting and nesting trees were taken down. Birds that used these trees had to go elsewhere and when they found a tree they liked, if a feeder was closer, I'm sure they went to that instead of coming back to mine.

When big, thick bushes are removed, species such as Gray Catbirds will move on to other yards.

Sometimes tree and shrub removal may cause certain species to leave, but other species may come in their place. For example, my mother had a heavily wooded backyard full of chickadees, titmice, brown thrashers and woodpeckers. A tornado came through and several trees were downed. When that happened, her bird activity was comparatively low and even after a year she didn't see brown thrashers in her yard and not nearly as many woodpeckers as before. The following spring, she did have a new bird show up in her yard: an Eastern Towhee. Due to some clearing of tall trees and creation of brush piles nearby, a pair of towhees found it an ideal spot for a nest and raised two young that Mom got to watch. So, sometimes you lose some, but may win some in exchange.

» **Lawns.** For years, an ideal yard was considered to be a well mowed grass lawn. From a bird's point of view, this is a very boring yard. Grass has no nutritional value whatsoever to birds. In addition, chemicals used to treat lawns are potentially fatal to birds. Many birds eat insects as well as seeds so killing off insects in your grass is also eliminating an important food source. This doesn't mean you have to turn your yard from a well landscaped scene to a chaotic-looking mini prairie, but finding organic solutions and incorporating bird friendly plants will be a big help. See pages 58-59 for bird friendly plants.

Apartment Birder Tip

You may not have a lawn, but environmentally friendly plant care also applies to planters, window boxes and container gardens. Organic methods of fertilizing and weed control are healthier for birds, and a few insects here and there will provide meals for a variety of feathered visitors.

CHAPTER TWO

Special Concerns for Apartment, Townhome and Condo Dwellers

Many people live in apartments, condominiums and townhomes. If you enjoy feeding the birds and are about to move into this type of living quarters, ask up front if they allow bird feeders. Don't just rely on seeing a bird feeder on someone's deck; always ask first and find out what the policy is.

Keeping your feeding area clean is important in any yard, but it is especially important when living in a condo or apartment setting. You may enjoy the birds, but your neighbors on the next floor down may not appreciate the mess that can build up. Make sure to keep in communication with your neighbors about your feeding. Find out if they have any concerns and if you can address them before they get angry, complain to the building manager, and set the process in motion to ban bird feeding in your complex.

Easy steps to help keep your area clean

A large tray under a feeder will help keep some of the mess off the ground, but not all of it.

1. Feed seed out of the shell such as sunflower chips, cracked corn and peanuts out of the shell. This will help cut down on the empty seed shells that can build up under a feeder. If you must feed seeds in the shell, have large trays under the feeder to help catch the empty shells and sweep up often under the feeding area.

2. If you have a deck with wooden slats or railing, try spreading Astroturf or landscaping cloth around the deck to help catch some of the spillage.

Apartment Birder Tip

Hanging feeders work well suspended from window frames. However, when selecting one, keep it small. A large feeder will sway in the wind and could bang against your window.

Mice inevitably become an issue with bird feeding, but mice will show up anywhere, whether or not there is a bird feeder. When mice show up, and if they find a bird feeder, they will use it as a food source, just as any wild animal would. Keeping the area under the feeder swept up helps keep mice at bay. The best defense indoors is a cat.

If you don't want to clean under your feeders or don't have time, consider hiring one of the kids who lives in your complex. Perhaps they would be willing to earn ten dollars a week by taking an hour to rake up the leftovers under your feeder. If you are thinking that cleaning up under the feeder is too much of a commitment, consider how badly you want to feed the birds. If steps aren't taken to keep the feeding area clean, you can have angry neighbors and have your feeders taken away. Also, messy seed can lead to disease affecting your birds.

Shelled peanuts don't leave much of a mess under a feeder and are enjoyed by a variety of backyard visitors, including this Red-breasted Nuthatch.

Alternatives to Feeders

If you are in a complex that already forbids bird feeding or has just told you to take down your feeders, you still have some options. First, talk to the building manager about setting up a community feeder. Is there a central spot where most of the residents can look at birds? Would it be feasible to set up a feeding station there?

If that is not an option, talk to the property managers or owners about the possibility of putting in plants that attract birds. Plants can attract birds that don't typically come to seed feeders and you can see some great birds year-round. There are several trees, shrubs and plants that can provide either cover or food (see Chapter Four).

All birds, like this cardinal, enjoy a good bath to keep their feathers in top condition.

Talk to the property manager and owners about providing water in the form of a pond or fountain. Birds need water year-round and are attracted by the sound of moving water. Small pond formats are limitless. People in your complex will not only enjoy the relaxing sounds of the fountain but may even appreciate the added benefits of the wildlife that it attracts. Not every bird eats seeds, but all birds need water.

Finally, look into the option of setting up bird houses. If it's a complex with wide open space, Eastern Bluebirds and Tree Swallows could be attracted with housing in warm weather. In more wooded areas, House Wrens and Black-capped Chickadees are welcome neighbors that might use nest boxes (see Chapter Seven).

How High is Too High?

Once you get above two stories above the top of the tree line, you may be too high to attract many birds. Rock Pigeons seem to perch anywhere and can always be attracted but they can be messy feeder guests. You will not attract cardinals, chickadees or nuthatches. If you live in a high-rise

Pergrine falcons prefer to nest high on a building like a skycraper.

there might be a potential for setting up a Peregrine Falcon nest box. Plans can be found on the Internet, but it is always best to partner with your state's wildlife management agency and definitely get the building manager's or owner's permission. While it is incredibly cool to have a peregrine nest on a building, neighbors who live below the nest box might not be thrilled by the occasional splash of peregrine poop or petrified pigeon parts that fall out of a nest box.

Attracting Birds On The Sly

If your building or complex does not allow bird feeding and the staff is not amenable to offering a feeding station in the complex, you might have to get creative. Keep in mind that if you have been told to not feed birds in your complex and you try to sneak the food to the birds, you are risking eviction or fines.

If you are going to try it, avoid putting obvious food out on the deck and avoid anything that looks like a bird feeder. Try putting out some plants on the deck, in the winter, spruce tops make a nice roosting area for sparrows. You can't help it if the birds use the plant as an area to perch. You might put non-germinating seed like sunflower hearts or peanuts on top the dirt. It will take a while for birds to notice this.

Window boxes can be attractive to American Robins, Mourning Doves, Carolina Wrens or Brown Thrashers as nesting sites.

Even if you do not have a deck, you can put planter boxes out on your windows and fill those with flowers and if you have wooden window frames, you could screw in hooks that will allow for hanging plant baskets. You can sneak in seeds out of the shell there as well. Keep in mind that it may take a while to get birds to notice that food is in there. If you are going to sneak food in there, always make sure that it is seed out of the shell, so no telltale signs are left behind.

If you want to avoid putting any type of food on the deck, consider adding a decorative water feature. If there is an outdoor outlet or if you can find a solar powered or battery operated pump, put it in a shallow dish and set that outside. Birds are attracted by the sound of moving water. By having a small decorative fountain with relaxing bubbling sounds, you will find that it will attract birds from all over the neighborhood. The advantage here is that you will attract more varieties of birds. Some species do not eat seed and will never come to a feeding station, but all birds need moisture in some form and the easiest way for them to find it is to listen for the sound of running water.

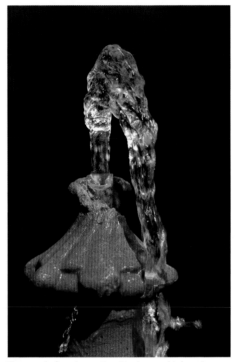

The sound of moving water attracts more bird species than any other item.

Look around for unique items that can be turned into a safe nesting box. For years, there was a company that turned old cowboy boots into functional wren houses which worked well, so look for the unexpected.

These painted gourds do not look like obvious nest boxes.

I would start with your local wild bird specialty store and see what they suggest for bird houses that do not look like a traditional house, but more like a work of art. Look up bird house plans in books and let your imagination run loose on the design.

Never underestimate the power of a hanging plant basket full of impatiens. You might get hummingbirds coming in for the nectar, but you

might also find that a House Finch, robin, Carolina Wren, or cardinal is nesting in the center of the basket. Consider adding artificial floral wreaths and vines as a decorative accent around the deck rail or windows, House Finches like to nest in that as well.

A hanging basket of imaptiens can be food for hummingbirds or a nest site for House Finches.

Location, Location, Location: Setting Bird Feeders in Your Yard or on Your Deck

Now it's time to figure out what types of systems you are going to use to place feeders in your yard. Remember, you'll want to set feeders where you can enjoy watching them.

OPPOSITE: A well-rounded feeding station.

Plan A: Pole Systems

The easiest way to mount your bird feeders is usually a pole system. Keep in mind that squirrels and raccoons can and will climb any pole (yes, even a skinny half-inch pole). You will need to purchase a type of squirrel and raccoon guard—often referred to as a baffle—to keep critters out.

A "shepherd's hook"-style pole makes it easy to remove feeders for refilling.

You get what you pay for when it comes to bird feeding poles. For bird feeding, look for a pole that you can easily adjust or take apart. Get a pole for which you can easily find additional parts. You may start out with two feeders and think that you only need two hooks on a pole, but you may decide to add more feeders down the road. Getting a pole that is easy to add parts to is essential.

Look closely at the quality of the pole. I have heard too many times from people who purchased a cheaper shepherd's hook pole only to discover too late that the gaps between the hooks are wide enough for a bird to slide its foot into and become stuck with lethal results.

Place the top of your squirrel and raccoon baffle at least five feet high on the pole, so the critters can't jump past it.

A variety of feeders can be hung together on one pole.

Height is very important when selecting a pole. The average squirrel can jump five feet vertically and ten feet horizontally—and that's just the average squirrels, not the Olympiad squirrels that some people insist they have.

A good pole should be seven to eight feet high. This gives you the necessary space to mount a baffle on the pole so that the top of it can hang five feet up and there is space enough above the baffle for feeders to hang. If your feeders hang below the baffle, that could allow an enterprising squirrel to climb the pole part of the way and jump over to grasp the feeder. I know that someone is reading this now and thinking, "they really wouldn't do that, would they?" but there's not much a squirrel won't do when food is involved.

You may be thinking, "Holy cow, Batman, if my pole is that tall, how will I ever get my feeders down to fill or clean them?" Most feeders are long enough that you will be able to grab them from the bottom and lift them off of their hooks. If you are a shorty like me and cannot reach the feeders, get a long hook—the kind they use at clothing stores to get clothes hanging off the walls—or add a cup hook to the end of an old broomstick and use that to reach the feeders. There's also a hook that I am awfully fond of called the Easy Lift Hanger. It's a silver hook with a

These feeders are hung with Easy Lift Hooks. The hooks have a curl so you can use a broom handle to hang them higher—perfect for short people trying to hang feeders up high!

corkscrew in the center that a broom handle fits into. You use the broom handle to raise and lower the hook off of the pole.

If you have a large platform-type feeder that needs to be mounted on a pole you will need a flange that fits on the bottom of the feeder and attaches to a pole. For this type of feeder, you only need a pole that is five and a half feet to six feet tall like in the lower left photo.

The top of a pole mounted baffle should be 5 feet.

Squirrels generally don't like the taste of Nyjer thistle, so you *may* not need a squirrel baffle for your goldfinch feeder.

Not only is it important to have your pole high, it's also important that you have it in the open. Squirrels can jump ten feet horizontally, so you have to make sure that there is nothing—and I mean nothing—within ten feet of the feeder. Squirrels will use a variety of things from which to project themselves. This includes, but is not limited to, bushes, shrubs, trellises, deck rails, fences, dog houses, your dog, garages, your house, small children, other bird feeder poles, lawn furniture, grills, your Aunt Tilly—get the idea?

Some people like the look of a wooden 4 x 4 post and these usually work well with really large feeders. You could use these to mount your bird feeders but be sure to use a squirrel and raccoon baffle on the pole to keep those critters from climbing it.

Remember, in order for a baffle to be effective, the top of it needs to be five feet above the ground and the pole needs to be at least eight to ten

This is a great example of how to pest-proof your feeding stations. The feeders are at least six feet off the ground; the 4 x 4 post has a raccoon/squirrel baffle six feet high; and there is nothing within ten feet of the post for a squirrel to use as a launching pad.

feet from a squirrel launching pad such as a deck railing or tree.

If trees and shrubs are too close to the feeder, you will need to prune them. If this is not an option, you may have to go for Plan B.

Plan B: Hanging Feeders in Trees

It is possible to hang bird feeders from trees and still keep critters out of them. Hanging baffles can be effective at keeping squirrels and raccoons off. Make sure that the bottom of the bird feeder doesn't hang lower than five feet and keep the feeder as far from the trunk of the tree as possible.

Another option is to string a wire between two trees and hang the feeders high in the air. The theory is that squirrels cannot navigate the wire. I know some customers for whom this has worked, but I have seen too many squirrels walk power lines and fear that it is only a matter of time before the squirrels start walking the wire.

If hanging the feeders in a tree with a baffle over the top doesn't work, then you will want to consider a weight-sensitive feeder. More on this in Chapter Nine.

Any dish with a smooth surface made of plastic, glass or pottery will prevent live mealworms from escaping. You can usually put mealworm feeders anywhere without a baffle. They are not high on the squirrel food preference list.

This setup looks safe, but isn't. A hungry squirrel could still jump from the deck rail to the feeder, then hang on for a stolen meal.

Deck Mounting

A variety of hook options are available for people to put on their decks. You can get a basic clamp-on shepherd's hook, a bracket that will attach to the rods of your deck rail, or brackets that will screw into a wooden deck rail. Some brackets will extend out about five feet to keep seed and bird droppings from accumulating on the deck.

Mounting feeders to your deck and getting only birds and not squirrels is very difficult to do. It is practically impossible to keep squirrels and raccoons from climbing onto decks, let alone keeping them off feeders. Squirrels will climb any deck bracket and jump from the deck railing to the feeder. Most raccoons are large enough that they simply lean over and grab what they want from the feeder.

If that last paragraph hasn't discouraged you from deck feeding, or if that is the only option available to you, there are a few techniques to try. Use bird feeders that are less likely to get a squirrel or raccoon's attention, such as a finch feeder (Nyjer is not popular with squirrels or raccoons). Finches are small birds and fairly tolerant of people. Feeding safflower can attract a nice variety of birds and the bitter-tasting seed will often be ignored by squirrels and raccoons. Most of the time squirrels will leave nectar and fruit feeders alone and you can get away with those types of feeders

Cup hooks are great for hanging nectar feeders for a variety of species including Baltimore Orioles.

A weight-sensitive feeder like the Eliminator is your best bet for keeping squirrels from raiding feeders mounted on decks.

hanging off of the deck. However, raccoons love the sweet stuff so you will want to take those feeders in at night.

If you want to use a weight-sensitive feeder to foil the squirrels, make sure that the deck bracket you are using hangs the feeder out far enough so a squirrel can't just lean over and get the food out of the feeding ports without getting on the feeder.

There is a type of deck-mounting system that can be used with some degree of success for keeping raccoons and squirrels out. It's a bit more expensive, but when compared to the amount of food and damaged feeders you can go through when dealing with raccoons and squirrels, it's well worth it.

Start with a pipe about eighty inches long and secure it to the deck at the bottom and again along the deck rail. Add a raccoon baffle above the deck rail. The important part is that the pole is a good 36" above the deck rail. A canister type works best because it will not block the view of your bird feeder. Add an arm to the pipe above the raccoon baffle that sticks out at least twenty-four inches. This set-up will keep raccoons from getting to the feeder. It will not keep squirrels out as they are nimble enough to jump on any feeder you hang on the hook. However, if you add a weight-sensitive feeder, this should take care of the squirrels and solve your critter problem.

With its sizable baffle and four-foot extended arm, this deck-mounted feeder is very difficult for squirrels and raccoons to reach.

Window Mounting

Birds will come right up to the windows. You can purchase feeders with suction cups or attach brackets to your window frames. Another option is to use a cup hook on a soffit above the window or hang feeders with hooks from gutters. Depending on the type of house you have or how close tree branches are to

Suction cup feeders bring birds up close and don't require the purchase of a pole or deck bracket.

windows you may or may not have a problem with squirrels. Raccoons do not have the gripping ability that squirrels do, so they generally will not climb up the side of a building to get at a feeder.

CHAPTER FOUR

Setting the Table

The type of bird food you use will greatly affect the types of birds you attract. If you have had a bird feeder for a while and have not attracted the colorful birds you were expecting, I will wager money that the bird food in your feeder is probably mostly yellow in color. If it is, that tells me that your bird food mix contains mostly white millet and cracked corn, which can be very useful in moderation at the right time of year, but are not ideal for a tube feeder.

OPPOSITE: Downy Woodpecker feeding on a seed cake held together with gelatin.

You can have fun and experiment with different foods in your backyard. When you are just getting started feeding birds, it's best to begin with feeding black-oil sunflower seed by itself or a mixture that is mostly sunflower. This will get you the most variety of birds. From there, if there is a bird species that you are not seeing that you would like to attract, experiment with different foods and mixes. Remember that if the habitat is not right for the bird, no amount of tasty food will attract it to your feeder.

Keep in mind that birds are creatures of habit; they don't like change. Sometimes people will switch from feeding sunflower mixes to straight safflower in the summertime to reduce the number of blackbirds at the feeder. Such a drastic change can cause all the birds to leave the feeder for anywhere from a week to four weeks.

It's like going to Wendy's to get a number one hamburger combo and they tell you that they are now a sushi restaurant and the number one combo

While on vacation at Virginia Beach, I put some oyster crackers out to see what birds would come. To my surprise, this catbird loved them!

is a salmon roll. It's not that you don't love sushi, but you were really in the mood for a hamburger and that's what you were expecting. Eventually, your love of sushi takes over and you're a regular customer again.

Basic Truths of Bird Feeding

More birds eat black-oil sunflower seed than any other seed.

Small birds not only eat small seeds but are very capable of eating very large seeds and nuts.

Birds are creatures of habit and if you dramatically switch the types of feed in your feeder you can freak them out.

Birds never need you to feed them. That is an urban legend that has proved to be untrue. Even in blizzard conditions, birds use a bird feeding station for only 20 percent of their diet. They treat feeding stations the way we should treat a fast food restaurant.

If you don't want bird seed germinating, purchase bird food that has been hulled or out of the shell.

Where to Buy Your Seed

Since birds live outdoors and endure much harsher living conditions than we do, people tend to assume that any old seed will do for birds. However, birds will not eat every seed that is put out for them. Where you get your bird seed can make a difference. I can't tell you the number of times I've had someone tell me that they found a really big bag of bird seed for an incredibly low price and then their birds disappeared when offered that seed. Chances are the seed was incredibly old and stale or full of filler seeds that birds don't care for.

Bird seed can be purchased in a variety of places but you want to make sure that you are getting the freshest and best seed possible for your dollar. Bird food specialty stores tend to have their food delivered frequently, so it's generally fresh and rotated. Larger stores such as hardware or discount retailers will purchase bird seed in huge quantities at a greatly reduced price, but won't order more until the order is all gone, regardless if that takes three months or a year and a half to sell it.

One thing to watch for when you are looking over a retailer's seed selection are Indian Meal Moths. One moth flying around bird food is understandable. A few eggs and larvae can get mixed in even when the seed is delivered fresh. Three to six moths buzzing around the bird seed is a warning that the food is not only a little old but infested with meal moth larvae. That is usually a signal that the retailer offering the bird food is not taking steps to keep meal moths from getting the seed or rotating the seed supply regularly for freshness.

Also, take a good look at the seed before purchasing it. A bag may say "Premium Songbird Mix" but that may be mostly millet and milo with just a handful of sunflowers. A reputable bird seed supplier will have a way for you to see what the mix looks like before you buy it.

Wild Bird Specialty Stores

I recommend purchasing your seed from a wild bird specialty store such as a Wild Birds Unlimited, Inc., Wild Bird Center or Wild Bird Store. For the most part, these stores are run by people who fanatically enjoy bird feeding and can give you expert advice for your yard. Everyone who works there will have tried out many of the feeders and can tell you firsthand of their experiences. They will tell you which foods they like and share stories from other customers. If you are unsure whether you have a wild bird specialty store nearby, go to www.wbu.know-where.com/wbu for a Wild Birds Unlimited, Inc., a company found across the United States and Canada.

Sometimes bird specialty stores don't have an obvious name like "wild bird" in the title. Some creative bird store names I have seen include Cardinal Corner, Chickadee Depot and Birds I View. You can try looking in the pet store section of your phone book or online directory, since that is usually the category wild bird stores are under.

Storing Bird Food

You will need storage containers for your bird food at home. A metal container like a galvanized steel trash can with lid or popcorn tins work really well. Avoid plastic because critters can chew through it. Even house mice can chew through hard plastic.

Storing bird seed inside your home can lead to an Indian Meal Moth infestation. These moths can be found in a variety of products including pet

Goldfinches tend not to eat Nyjer thistle that is more than six months old. Purchase fresh—and often. (Droll Yankees model #CJTHM15Y)

food and bird seed. Once bird seed has left the distributing warehouse it's a good bet that there will be meal moth eggs and larvae in the seed by the time it reaches the bird store. There's no safe chemical to put in the seed that would kill the moth, but not harm birds at the same time. Some distributors try to help by freezing seed before it reaches a retail outlet, but that may not kill all the eggs.

If eggs and larvae are in the seed it can be a bonus of extra protein for the birds. However, if the larvae and eggs sit too long, they can multiply and begin to cocoon. When this happens, your bird seed gets webby and clumps together, making it difficult to move through the bird feeder. Also, the larvae will eat the nutmeat inside the shells, making the seed less desirable to your birds.

When buying bird seed always try to buy the freshest seed possible. When you find a load of seed at a tremendous discount, be wary; the reason could be old seed. Some seeds can stay fresh after a year, but the nutmeat does begin to shrink and if your neighbors are offering fresher seed, the birds will visit them before they visit you.

Apartment Birder Tip

If you must store seed in your home keep it in the refrigerator or freezer and purchase it in small quantities to always keep it fresh. In the best of all possible worlds you should store your seed in your garage, in a metal container with a tight lid.

Appetizing Foods for Birds

New menu items for birds show up all the time. Included here are some of the basics and some of the newer types of foods being offered in stores for birds.

Single Seed Types

black-oil sunflower

» Black Oil Sunflower Seed: Black-oil sunflower seed, or "oilers" as they are sometimes called, are the preferred seed of birds in the U.S. Birds from large cardinals to tiny chickadees enjoy them because of their high fat content and easy-to-strip-away shells. The seeds can be fed by themselves or in a mix. A good all-purpose bird food mix uses the black-oil sunflower seed as its base.

striped sunflower

» Striped Sunflower Seed: Not as popular at most feeders as the black-oil sunflower, striped sunflower seed, also called "stripes," are enjoyed by many bird species. It is a larger sunflower seed with a tougher shell, readily eaten by Northern Cardinals and Blue Jays, but even a Black-capped Chickadee or Tufted Titmouse is capable of cracking open the shell of this seed.

sunflower chips

sunflower hearts

» Hulled Sunflower (non-germinating): Sunflower seeds can be offered completely out of the shell as either the whole nutmeat (called a heart) or ground into chips. Birds seem to prefer this over any other form of seed. The advantage is that you will not have an accumulation of empty seed shells under the feeder when you use hulled sunflower, nor will it germinate. The disadvantage is that starlings, which are unable to eat hard-shelled black-oil sunflower seeds, will devour sunflower chips. Every seed-eating bird will eat hulled sunflower seeds. Also, this seed is more apt to get moldy in wet and humid weather.

safflower

» Safflower: This seed resembles a white black-oil sunflower seed and can be fed in mixes or by itself. One of the advantages of safflower is that usually squirrels, starlings, grackles and crows will leave it alone. If safflower is fed in a mix, it will sometimes be the last seed eaten by the birds. But when fed by itself, it will attract cardinals, Rose-breasted Grosbeaks, Mourning Doves, House Finches, chickadees, Tufted Titmice and nuthatches. Because this seed is unattractive to squirrels and blackbirds it works very well in platform style feeders.

white millet

» White Millet: White millet is not the most popular seed on the planet, but is very important to have on hand in winter and during migration for fun sparrows (yes, I said fun) like Harris's Sparrows, White-throated Sparrows, White-crowned Sparrows, Song Sparrows and Dark-eyed Juncos. If you are the type of person who says, "I don't care how cool they are, I really don't need another brown bird at my feeder," let me tempt you with this little fact: Indigo Buntings love white millet. Yes, it's true, one of the most beautiful and coveted birds out there loves to eat millet. The best time to try to attract buntings is during migration, especially before insects are out in full force and birds are looking for alternate sources of food on their journey. It is fine as a small part of a bird seed mix but white millet should not be the main ingredient. Most birds tend to kick it out in favor of other seeds, so it's best to offer it on the ground or in a low-hanging platform feeder. Other birds that will eat white millet include House Sparrows, Tree Sparrows, Carolina Wrens, Eastern Towhees and Mourning Doves.

cob corn

cracked corn

shelled or whole corn

» Corn: Corn can be offered cracked, whole kernel or on the cob. Corn will attract Mallards, Canada Geese, Wild Turkeys, Ring-necked Pheasants, squirrels, rabbits, deer and doves. This food can be offered by scattering it on the ground or nailing cobs down. Many people use corn as bribery for the squirrel union in their backyards. Like millet, the birds that tend to eat corn are ground feeders. Cracked corn will go to waste in a tube feeder and whole kernel corn will get stuck. Cracked and whole kernel corn is best served on a low hanging tray feeder or on the ground.

mixed nuts

peanuts in shell

mixed nuts

» Peanuts/Mixed Nuts: Many people fear that offering nuts in their yard will bring squirrels to the feeder. Squirrels love sunflower seed just as much as they love nuts, so whether you offer nuts or not, squirrels are going to show up unless you live on Mars. Nuts can be offered out of the shell in mesh feeders where birds have to peck at them and fly away with the peanut pieces, as an ingredient in bird food mixes or scattered on a tray or deck railing. Just about every bird species eats nuts, including chickadees, nuthatches and cardinals. Blue Jays are particularly fond of nuts and many people enjoy offering them peanuts in the shell. If you watch a Blue Jay closely with a pile of mixed nuts, it will pick one up and drop it. It will repeat this two more times. Studies have shown that Blue Jays are testing to find out which one is heaviest and likely contains the most nutmeat. Whichever nut is the heaviest, the Blue Jay will fly away with that one.

Nyjer

» Nyjer: This tiny seed has a complicated background. Nyjer was originally spelled niger because it was grown in Nigeria. When it was brought over to the United States some people mispronounced the name. The seed was then given the folk name thistle. Unfortunately, many people confuse it with thistles—some of which are noxious—so the Wild Bird Feeding Industry has made a move to spell it phonetically: Nyjer. Whew!

Finches adore Nyjer. Believe it or not, finches do crack open an outer hull to eat the nutmeat on the inside, so when you feed Nyjer there will be an accumulation of shells on the ground. Keep in mind that this seed has a limited shelf life. Most seed, when kept in a cool dry place, can be used almost two years after it's harvested. However, once Nyjer is six months old, finches will not eat it.

pumpkin seeds

» Pumpkin Seeds: Pumpkin seeds are showing up in more and more mixes. They can be fed on their own or added to bird seeds. They sometimes get stuck in tube style feeders so they usually work best in a platform style feeder or wooden feeders. Pumpkin seeds are enjoyed by Northern Cardinals, Blue Jays, Tufted Titmice, Black-capped Chickadees and a variety of woodpeckers and turkeys.

Mixes

typical mix

» ***All-Purpose Mix:*** This is an all-purpose sunflower mix. It is mostly black-oil sunflower seeds, which most birds prefer. There are a variety of other seeds including peanuts, cracked corn, white millet and safflower. This is sure to attract a huge variety of birds.

inferior mix

» ***Crap Mix:*** This mix is mostly yellow and orange, indicating that it is full of white millet and milo. Unless you have a flock of quail in your yard, you will not be getting much activity at the milo. This mix is best fed on the ground or, even better, not at all in the eastern U.S.

clean mix

» ***Non-Germinating Mix:*** This is a mixture of hulled sunflower seeds, peanuts and cracked corn. This is a nice variety of seeds for just about every seed-eating bird out there and it will not germinate.

thistle sunflower chips

Finches' Feast

» ***Finch Mix:*** Finches will eat a variety of foods. Two of their favorite seeds are Nyjer and sunflower chips. The chips in this mix are ground so fine that they will fit through the small slits of a finch feeder. Other seeds that finches enjoy include flax, canary seed, canola seed and hulled millet. This type of mix is nice to scatter on the ground during migration for native sparrows such as White-crowned Sparrows, Fox Sparrows and Harris's Sparrows.

gourmet mix

» ***Gourmet Mix:*** Here is a fancy mix for fancy birds. This mix has sunflower seed—both in the shell and out of the shell—pumpkin seeds, dried fruits and mixed nuts. Guaranteed to delight the palates of catbirds, cardinals or even robins. That is, if you can keep the other birds away.

Other Options

nut suet cake   suet pellets   inferior suet   suet plugs or logs

» Suet: Suet is rendered beef fat and can be provided in a number of ways. Woodpeckers, chickadees and nuthatches go nuts for it. You can purchase chunks of beef fat in grocery stores or cakes and plugs of rendered suet in various flavors and textures. Non-rendered suet is best fed in winter; it will melt and go rancid in the heat of summer. Birds do seem to prefer flavored suets, especially if they are flavored with nuts, peanut butter or sunflower seeds. Suet can also be purchased in the form of non-melting doughs and can be fed year-round. You can offer suet in cages of various shapes and sizes, crumbled on trays, or smeared into tree bark or special log-style feeders with prepared holes for suet plugs. Beware of suet full of millet and corn—it tends to be left uneaten.

mealworms   waxworms

» Mealworms: Just about every bird eats mealworms. You can provide them as an extra snack at your bird feeders or you can set up small cups near bluebird houses and fill them with mealworms for bluebirds. Mealworms can be purchased roasted or live. Birds will eat either, but they prefer live wiggly ones. You can offer waxworms but birds prefer mealworms. They're best offered in a smooth-surfaced cup or tray.

» Fresh Fruit: Many people have heard that orange halves are a fun food to offer in spring for orioles. Other birds such as House Finches, catbirds, woodpeckers and robins will utilize this citrus fruit as well. But you don't have to stop there. Grapefruit halves can be offered, as well as cut up pieces of apples, grapes, cherries, strawberries and blueberries. When pomegranates are in season they can be offered, much to the delight of cardinals. In warm weather you can let the fruit get old; it will attract hummingbirds who will eat the fruit flies that are attracted to the overripe fruit. Don't worry, birds know enough not to eat moldy fruit.

gourmet mixes

» Dried Fruit: Many bird seed mixes contain dried fruit such as raisins, dried cranberries, dried pineapple and dried papaya. Some bird food even has fruit flavoring in it. These are just some extra snacks you can provide. Dried fruit pieces are best offered on trays.

grape jelly

» Grape Jelly: The secret to getting a Baltimore Oriole's attention and loyalty is grape jelly. They absolutely love it, especially when they first return from migration. Some of my customers have had as many as six orioles waiting in line at the feeder to get at grape jelly. Gray Catbirds, House Finches and Red-bellied Woodpeckers are also fond of jelly. In my opinion, it's best to use regular Welch's or Smucker's jelly. Some of my customers have found that the fancy organic jelly is not to the orioles' liking.

nectar

» Nectar: Nectar is primarily for hummingbirds and orioles, although woodpeckers or House Finches have been known to partake of it as well. You can make nectar at home or you can purchase it. The recipe for basic hummingbird nectar mimics the sugar solution found naturally in plants. Take four parts water and one part table sugar and boil it until the sugar is dissolved. Do not use honey or artificial sweetener; only use table sugar. After the nectar has cooled, pour it into the feeder and the rest can be stored in the refrigerator for up to two weeks.

You can purchase powdered nectar or sugar solution concentrate at the store that is perfectly fine to use and quite frankly is much easier. You don't have to boil commercial nectar and in the case of the liquid concentrate you don't have stir it nearly as much.

There is an urban legend that says the red dye in hummingbird nectar is potentially fatal. It has never been scientifically proven to be true or false. There are anecdotal stories, but the bottom line is that there's no proof either way. Most hummingbird feeders have enough red on them, so red nectar isn't needed anyway.

You can purchase oriole nectar separately, but in many commercial nectars the only difference between the hummingbird and oriole is the color. There are a few that are orange flavored but for the most part there is no difference in the amount of sugar between the two. It's best to err on the side of caution and keep nectar clear.

There is some debate as to how much sugar you should use. Some argue that during migration the sugar solution should be higher than four to one, but all that will do is cause the orioles and hummingbirds to visit the feeder less often. The birds fill up on sugar faster and won't stay as long. Plus, there is a risk for dehydration. So to be on the safe side, stick with four to one, that is the closest sugar solution to what is found in nectar rich flowers.

Keeping nectar and jelly fresh is essential. If nectar is in direct sun it can go bad after two days. If it's in the shade, it can go bad after five days. If you don't keep up with keeping the nectar fresh, the hummingbirds will ignore you. Think of it as a can of soda. Would you still drink from an open can of soda that had been sitting in direct sun for three days in a row? Hummingbirds and orioles won't either. Watch for black mold and fungus. If you see black in corners and crevices that is fungus and the feeder needs to be cleaned. If the nectar looks cloudy that is another sign it needs to be cleaned.

» **Eggshells:** During breeding season female birds go through a lot of calcium to produce eggs. Some birds will eat the eggshells after their chicks hatch to replace it. You can help this process by offering crushed eggshells on tray feeders. You may be surprised by what shows up for eggshells; like Purple Martins. There is some concern that salmonella can be transmitted this way, so if you are going to offer eggshells to birds, make sure to microwave the shells for one minute or bake the shells at 250° for half an hour before offering them outside.

Baltimore Orioles have a "sweet beak" in spring and will come to oranges, grape jelly and nectar, but switch to insects when the chicks hatch.

Food Preferences

	MOST LIKELY TO EAT ◉ KINDA' LIKELY TO EAT ◉ HIGHLY UNLIKELY TO EAT ○	black oil sunflower	striped sunflower	hulled sunflower	safflower	white millet	cracked corn	whole corn	peanuts	peanuts in the shell	mixed nuts	Nyjer
EASY TO ATTRACT												
	Cardinal, Northern	●	●	●	●	●	●	○	●	○	●	○
	chickadees	●	●	●	●	●	●	○	●	●	●	●
	Dove, Mourning	●	●	●	●	●	●	●	●	○	●	●
	Duck, Wood	◐	◐	◐	●	●	●	●	●	○	◐	○
	Finch, House	●	●	●	●	●	●	○	●	○	●	○
	Goldfinch, American	●	◐	●	○	○	○	○	○	○	○	●
	Hawk, Cooper's	○	○	○	○	○	○	○	○	○	○	○
	Hawk, Red-tailed	○	○	○	○	○	○	○	○	○	○	○
	Hawk, Sharp-shinned	○	○	○	○	○	○	○	○	○	○	○
	Junco, Dark-eyed	●	○	●	○	●	●	○	●	○	○	●
	Mallard	●	◐	●	●	●	●	●	●	○	●	○
	nuthatches	●	●	●	●	●	●	○	●	●	●	○
	orioles	○	○	●	○	○	○	○	○	●	●	○
	Pheasant, Ring-necked	●	●	●	●	●	●	●	●	●	●	○
	Robin, American	○	○	●	○	○	○	○	●	○	●	○
	Sparrow, Chipping	●	○	●	○	●	●	○	●	○	●	●
	Sparrow, Song	●	○	●	○	●	●	○	●	○	●	●
	Titmouse, Tufted	●	●	●	●	●	○	○	●	●	●	●
	woodpeckers	●	●	●	○	○	○	○	●	●	●	●
	Wren, Carolina	●	○	●	○	●	●	○	●	○	●	○
	Wren, House	○	○	○	○	○	○	○	○	○	○	○
CHALLENGE TO ATTRACT												
	Bluebird, Eastern	○	○	●	○	○	○	○	●	○	●	○
	Bunting, Indigo	●	○	●	○	●	●	○	●	○	○	●
	Catbird, Gray	○	○	●	○	○	○	○	●	○	●	○
	Grosbeak, Rose-breasted	●	●	●	●	●	○	○	●	○	●	○
	Hummingbird, Ruby-throated	○	○	○	○	○	○	○	○	○	○	○
	Kestrel, American	○	○	○	○	○	○	○	○	○	○	○
	Killdeer	○	○	○	○	○	○	○	○	○	○	○
	Sparrow, White-throated	●	○	●	○	●	●	○	○	○	○	●
	Thrasher, Brown	●	○	●	●	●	○	○	●	○	●	○
	towhees	●	○	●	○	●	●	○	●	○	●	○
	Turkey, Wild	●	●	●	●	●	●	●	●	●	●	○
TOO MANY=PAIN!												
	Blackbird, Red-winged	●	●	●	●	●	●	●	●	○	●	○
	Crow, American	●	●	●	●	●	●	●	●	●	●	○
	Goose, Canada	●	●	●	●	●	●	●	●	●	●	○
	Grackle, Common	●	●	●	○	●	●	●	●	●	●	○
	Jay, Blue	●	●	●	●	●	●	●	●	●	●	○
	Mockingbird, Northern	●	○	●	○	●	●	○	○	●	●	○
	Pigeon, Rock	●	●	●	●	●	●	●	○	●	○	○
	Sparrow, House	●	●	●	●	●	●	○	●	○	●	○
	Starling, European	○	○	●	○	○	○	●	○	○	●	●

* Hummingbirds won't eat the fruit, but will eat the fruit flies

pumpkin seeds · all purpose mix · non-germinating mix · finch mix · gourmet mix · suet · mealworms · fresh fruit · dried fruit · grape jelly · egg shells · peanut butter · nectar · other birds · mammals under feeder

Plants for Birds

For food in summer some great plants are elderberry, Nanking cherry, serviceberry and pin cherry.

Other great fruit-bearing trees and shrubs for small yards include chokecherry, mountain-ash, black huckleberry, Northern bayberry, sand cherry, sumac, coralberry and lowbush blueberry.

Some plants produce berries that are bitter and undesirable when they first ripen in the fall. They sit on the plant all winter long and dry out, losing their moisture and keeping their sugar. These plants are valuable sources of food in late winter and early spring and include crab apple, sumac, bittersweet and highbush cranberry.

Offer flowers that go to seed in late summer and fall, such as sunflowers and petunias. Goldfinches love to perch on dead flowers and eat the seeds.

Some plants that are very attractive to hummingbirds include fuchsia, petunia, cardinal flower, honeysuckle, salvia, trumpet vine, scarlet bergamot, Impatiens and phlox.

Conifers such as pines, firs, spruces, cedars, arborvitae and junipers offer excellent cover for cardinals, sparrows, chickadees, doves and even owls in the winter.

It is possible to see American Robins all winter long, especially feeding on dried berries.

Bohemian Waxwings don't come to seed feeders but will show up in large numbers for berries in the northern part of the United States. In the South, watch for the similiar-looking Cedar Waxwing.They don't have a rusty colored vent.

Apartment Birder Tip

If you only have deck space to work with, try some container gardening—this is especially useful for bringing hummingbirds to your deck. The best part of attracting hummingbirds with plants is that you don't have to wash them out once or twice a week like you would a hummingbird feeder. I have had excellent luck attracting hummingbirds with nectaring flowers such as fuchsia, petunia, wax begonia, salvia, cardinal flower and impatiens. I don't have a particularly green thumb (I would give it the color olive at best), but I haven't managed to kill these plants. Cardinal climber was especially defiant and took over the whole window. All of these plants are ideal for hanging baskets or container gardening.

My sister grew petunias in her window box and let them go to seed in the fall. To her surprise, she had goldfinches fly in and eat all the seeds, so some of these plants can work for both nectar and seed.

Other good plants for container gardens include geranium, spotted jewelweed, French marigold, nasturtium and flowering tobacco.

Nectar-rich plants are a great option for people who want to attract hummingbirds but don't have time to keep a nectar feeder fresh and clean.

Bird Feeders

There is a huge variety of feeders out there. A good bird feeder will last you about four years. A fantastic feeder will last you fifteen years or more (yes, there are some that can last that long when properly taken care of). Take time when selecting feeders.

OPPOSITE: American Goldfinches

Spotting a Good Bird Feeder

You want something sturdy that has a warranty. Another important factor to keep in mind is how easy the feeder will be to clean. I know someone just read that passage and thought to themselves, "Clean the feeder? What do you mean 'clean the feeder?' I'm supposed to clean it too?" YES!

When selecting a feeder, look to see if the bottom twists or comes apart easily with screws so you can clean out leftover seed. Look at all the areas where seed is supposed to flow out for the birds. Will you be able to clean these ports easily? Will the seed be able to move out of the port easily? When it's rainy or if it's very humid, seed can get caked in there with fungus and you might need to clean it more

A clean feeder with fresh seed will attract more birds and prevent disease from spreading.

often than other bird feeders. Will the port or perches come out so you can have access to the inside of the feeder for cleaning? A good feeder will also come apart easily by removing a few screws. If the bird feeder doesn't come apart easily it's not worth the money—no matter how cute it is.

Some wild bird specialty stores offer a bird feeder cleaning program. When you purchase a bird feeder, ask if they are offering that service or if the employees have any tips for keeping feeders clean.

Another feature to look for is if the feeder is dishwasher safe. It is rare to find a dishwasher safe bird feeder; even feeders that have lifetime warranties against squirrel damage aren't always dishwasher safe. Plexiglas can melt or crack in hot water.

Squeaky Clean Feeders *(You're not running a greasy spoon)*

The mark of a good feeder is that it comes apart easily for cleaning.

Keeping feeders clean makes a huge difference in the number of birds visiting your feeders. Feeders should be cleaned at least once a month, any time you see sick birds at the feeder, after a good hard rain, if you notice chunks of bird food, white webbing around bird food, or if there is a foul odor. Dirty feeders will either spread disease and kill birds or keep birds from visiting your feeder.

To clean feeders you can purchase commercial products at bird stores, use anti-bacterial dish soap, or a mild solution of a capful of bleach to a gallon of water.

This is a bird danger zone. Dirty feeders with fecal matter plastered on old seed shells can become contaminated with salmonella, killing off visiting birds. If your feeders look like this, put down this book right now and clean them immediately!

What does a sick bird look like?

These are all possible symptoms and could be signs of West Nile Virus, pink eye or salmonella.

- Eyes half-closed
- Feathers fluffed
- Bird doesn't fly away when everyone else does
- Bird sleeping on the feeder
- You can approach within one foot or almost touch the bird without it noticing

House Finch with conjunctivitis

Wash all feeders immediately with bleach or antibacterial soap anytime you see sick birds or dead birds with no obvious injury. If you are not able to clean the feeder thoroughly, throw it away and purchase a feeder that can be easily cleaned. Remove all the seed that was in the feeder and on the ground and dispose of it in the trash. Any food you have left

White-breasted Nuthatch puffed out and not moving is a sign the bird could be sick.

in storage should be safe to use but any food that was outside with the feeders could be contaminated.

The chances of you catching a disease from a bird are incredibly slim. Most bird illnesses are not transmittable to mammals. The few diseases that are transmittable are avoidable if you practice basic hygiene such as wearing gloves when cleaning your feeders and washing your hands with antibacterial soap.

Platform Feeders

Platform bird feeders are the easiest way to provide bird seed and allow for a wide variety of birds. A platform feeder can be as simple as scattering seed on the ground or on top of a picnic table or stump. A good commercial model will have screening on the bottom to allow for drainage when it rains. There is a type of platform feeder with a roof that is called a fly-through platform. The roof is ideal since it helps keep rain and snow from building up in the feeders and birds appreciate the extra cover.

A "Fly-Thru" feeder is a platform with a roof, which helps keep rain and snow off the seed.

Most platform style feeders are made out of wood, which makes them difficult to clean and something for squirrels to chew on. There are newer models being made out of recycled plastic, which last much longer than cedar feeders and are much easier to keep clean. Platforms can be set on the ground and filled with white millet, cracked corn and sunflower hearts and are attractive

Ground-feeding trays keep seed elevated and if kept clean are a safe feeder for anything from House Finches to Wild Turkeys.

feeders for sparrows, juncos, Mourning Doves, cardinals, Carolina Wrens, Ring-necked Pheasants, ducks, geese and Wild Turkeys.

Platforms mounted higher in trees or on poles and filled with sunflower, peanuts, safflower, dried fruit or mealworms are ideal for cardinals, finches, Mourning Doves, Blue Jays, grosbeaks and House Finches.

Apartment Birder Tip

If pigeons are a problem in your area, avoid feeders with trays to make it difficult for them to land on the feeder and eat. You may consider using a weight sensitive feeder to keep pigeons away.

Wooden Hopper Feeders

Many recognize the traditional cedar bird feeders as an attractive accent that was in our grandparents' backyards. Wooden feeders can be ideal since they can hold large quantities of bird seed and have wide open perching areas for birds. This allows for several birds to feed at once and allows for larger species such as cardinals to feed.

Wooden feeders are traditional, but can be tougher to clean and have no warranties against squirrel damage.

Wooden feeders need to be well protected as the large perching area is an ideal spot for squirrels to sit and eat to their heart's content. Another problem is that squirrels have teeth that are constantly growing and they need something to chew on to help wear them down. What could be better then the roof of your cedar bird feeder?

Many people have wooden bird feeders and find great success with them. If you'd like to give them a try, just make sure that they are well protected from squirrels and raccoons.

This new take on the wooden hopper-style feeder is made out of durable recycled plastic, and accommodates a variety of birds such as juncos, house finches, goldfinches and cardinals.

All-Purpose Tube Feeders

An all-purpose tube feeder will have bigger ports for larger seed such as sunflowers. If you put Nyjer thistle in this feeder, it will blow out on a windy day.

Tube feeders with large, circular feeding ports are meant to be used as sunflower mix feeder and feed a large variety of birds.

Tube feeders have also come a long way in the last twenty years. The best ones come apart easily for cleaning, have squirrel damage warranties and metal perches. Good tube feeders also have the option of adding a tray. Trays are important if you want to attract cardinals, as these larger birds usually have a tougher time feeding from the perches on most tube feeders. Some people are concerned that adding a tray to a tube feeder makes it easier for squirrels to take over. If a squirrel wants the seed in the feeder bad enough, it will find a way to hang on a tube feeder whether there is a tray on it or not.

Trays on tube feeders have other advantages. Birds are messy eaters and a tray will catch some of the seed that gets spilled and some of the seed husks that fall as the birds are eating. Trays also allow for more birds to feed at a time, which can be incredibly helpful in the winter months when you get a ravenous flock of winter finches descending on your yard.

The Rose-breasted Grosbeak and other large birds feel more comfortable perching on feeders that have a tray, as opposed to a perch.

Finch Feeders

Tube feeders with small slits are meant to feed finch mixes such as Nyjer or extra fine sunflower chips. The birds that feed on Nyjer are tiny, so the small slits help keep some of the larger birds such as grackles from taking over the feeder since their bills are usually too big to fit inside the feeding port. Although, if it's a poorly designed feeder made of weak materials, sometimes blackbirds will enlarge the holes.

If you are not sure if you have finches in your area and are hesitant to invest in a tube feeder, you can purchase what's called a finch pouch. It's a refillable nylon bag with small holes that finches cling to. If you have finches in

Goldfinches appear attracted to the color yellow. Hanging a yellow feeder will increase your odds of attracting them.

your area and you hang out one of these bags, I guarantee they will show up. In winter months when finches are in large nomadic flocks, it's possible to have so many finches feeding that the pouch is invisible.

Finch feeders have smaller openings to accommodate their preferred foods of Nyjer thistle and fine sunflower chips. This also prevents birds with larger bills from taking the finch food.

Another handy finch feeder is the upside-down feeder. Some people want to attract goldfinches and only goldfinches. So tube feeders with feeding slits under the perches were developed. The theory is that goldfinches can figure this out relatively quickly; however House Finches and House Sparrows can figure it out, too. Whether or not you want to keep other birds away, it's worth it to have one in your yard just to watch a little yellow bird eat upside down.

Suet Feeders

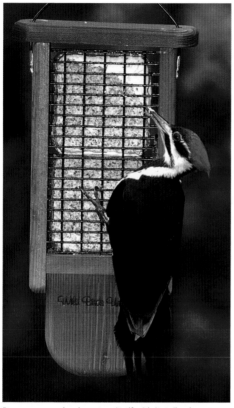

Because a woodpecker props itself with its tail, a large member of the family—such as the Pileated Woodpecker—will find tail props on the bottom of suet feeders helpful.

When putting suet into a log, press firmly or smush it. Otherwise woodpeckers may peck so hard that the suet falls out of the log.

Suet primarily attracts woodpeckers, chickadees and nuthatches; however, you can find Brown Creepers, orioles, catbirds, Carolina Wrens and warblers feeding on suet during an unexpected spring cold snap.

Suet feeders can be basic wire mesh cages that will hold pre-made cakes of rendered suets. You can also purchase or make your own suet log by simply drilling one-inch holes in an old tree log and jamming the holes full of suet. Since most of the birds that eat suet are able to cling, trays and perches are not necessary on suet feeders.

If you have small woodpeckers only, such as the Downy and Hairy Woodpeckers, a small single suet cake feeder is ideal. If you have the larger woodpeckers, such as the Red-bellied and Pileated Woodpeckers, you need to have a longer feeder. Think about woodpeckers for a moment. Whenever you see them, they are usually on the side of a tree

Upside-down suet feeders are no problem for woodpeckers, chickadees and nuthatches but are difficult for starlings, grackles and crows to raid.

with their tails propping them up. Without anything to prop their tails against, large woodpeckers have a tough time feeding on suet feeders. Some cake feeders include a wooden slat on the bottom of the feeder just to make it easier for larger woodpeckers to prop themselves up.

Suet feeders can be free-hanging or mounted onto the side of a tree or building. I don't recommend hanging suet from the side of a building. I used to hang mine on the side of my bedroom window ledge and one day it got warmer than I expected and the suet in my feeder dripped down and left a lovely grease stain on the bricks—ew. Another problem with mounting suet feeders on the sides of trees and buildings is that can make easier access for squirrels and raccoons to eat the suet.

Sometimes, I will take some extra suet and rub it on the sides of a tree in the winter for woodpeckers. The suet will get down into the nooks and crannies of the bark where woodpeckers can use their tongues to get at the food and squirrels have a tough time getting hold of it. This is especially handy if you are trying to take photos of woodpeckers and you want it to look like a natural setting.

Apartment Birder Tip

Avoid placing a suet feeder directly on or within 12 inches of a window. Birds manage to spray a fleck of suet whenever they pick at it. After a few weeks, the resulting greasy residue builds up into a hard-to-clean mess.

Wire Mesh Peanut/Black-Oil Sunflower Feeders

Mesh feeders are designed for shelled peanuts, which can be eaten even by small birds like the White-breasted Nuthatch.

You can also fill mesh feeders with black oil sunflower seeds.

These are wire mesh feeders that birds can cling to or perch on the trays at the bottom. The mesh easily holds peanuts out of the shell, mixed nuts or black-oil sunflower seeds. The mesh design makes these sturdy feeders that accommodate a wide variety of birds.

Fruit, Jelly and Mealworm Feeders

These are small glass, plastic or metal dishes that can be hung or mounted to a pole or deck. The primary intention is generally to attract orioles, but catbirds, woodpeckers, cardinals, House Finches and bluebirds will sometimes show up as well.

Bluebirds will come to feeders, but they must be "trained" to do it. Sometimes it's easier to start with a feeder that resembles a bluebird house—a shape with which they are familiar.

Bars help keep grackles and squirrels at bay, but an oriole can easily fit its head inside to get the jelly.

Place mealworms in glass, plastic or metal dishes, so the mealworms don't crawl out. Tufted Titmice love these juicy tidbits!

Nectar Feeders

Saucer-style nectar feeders are great because, unlike some of the more traditional feeders, they don't drip and are easier to keep clean.

A perch or not a perch—it doesn't matter to hummingbirds. Either way, they'll pay your feeder a visit.

Nectar feeders come in a huge variety of shapes and styles. The best styles tend to be the saucer type, which keep the nectar from spilling on windy days. Because nectar can ferment very quickly, it's important to get a feeder that is easy to clean. Hummingbirds and orioles will ignore a dirty feeder with fungus in it.

Another type is the dripper style. These are usually blown glass and very decorative feeders with a small tube and stopper with a hole at the end. There is a tiny amount of dripping with these feeders, hence the name dripper feeder, but they are attractive and hummingbirds will feed from them. They are often difficult to clean and it can be hard to find replacement stoppers if they fall out and get lost, which can leave a small sticky mess.

Suction Cup Window Feeders

Believe it or not, these can be great little feeders, especially if you have problems with birds flying into your windows. If you have a feeder directly on your window, birds will fly in slower to check out the food source. At first birds may be a little nervous around the window, but once they get used to the movement in the house they will readily visit the feeder. There are suction cup feeders for seed and nectar.

Try to put the window feeder up when it's above freezing. If it's cold, run your blow dryer on the window for a few minutes to warm it up. Make sure that your window is clean on the outside. The secret in getting window feeders to stick is usually on your face. Rub the suction cup on your nose (make sure not to be wearing any makeup or that can counteract the effects of your natural face oil). Then place the feeder on the window. Your natural face oil will help the suction cups stick better than saliva or cooking oil. Periodically, the suction cups will pop off. Most window feeders have more than one suction cup on them, so when you notice that one has come loose, take the feeder down, remove the suction cups and place them at a roiling boil in a pot of water for ten minutes. Let them cool on a paper towel and they should regain their shape. Wash them and clean off your window and rub some face oil on those suction cups and the feeder should be good to go. You should be able to reuse suction cups several times using this method.

Window-style feeders will dispense nectar or seed. (Droll Yankees model #WH-2 on left; W1 on right)

Tray-style window feeders attract the widest variety of birds. (Droll Yankees model #OWF)

Feeder Types and the Best Seed to Put in Them

MOST LIKELY TO ACCTRACT ●
KINDA' LIKELY TO ACCTRACT ◐
HIGHLY UNLIKELY TO ACCTRACT ○

	Platform	Wooden Hopper	All Purpose Tube	Finch	Suet	Wire Mesh	Oriole	Hummingbird	Window
Black-oil Sunflower	●	●	●	○	○	●	○	○	●
Striped Sunflower	●	●	◐	○	○	○	○	○	●
Hulled Sunflower	●	●	●	○	○	●	○	○	●
Extra Fine Sunflower Chips	●	◐	◐	●	○	○	○	○	○
Safflower	●	●	●	○	○	●	○	○	●
White Millet	●	◐	○	○	○	●	○	○	○
Cracked Corn	●	○	○	○	○	○	○	○	○
Whole Corn	●	○	○	○	○	○	○	○	○
Peanuts	●	◐	◐	○	○	●	○	○	●
Peanuts in the Shell	●	○	○	○	○	○	○	○	●
Mixed Nuts	●	◐	○	○	○	●	○	○	●
Nyjer	●	○	◐	●	○	○	○	○	●
Pumpkin Seeds	●	○	◐	○	○	○	○	○	●
All Purpose Mix	●	◐	●	○	○	◐	○	○	●
Non-Germinating Mix	●	◐	●	○	○	◐	○	○	●
Finch Mix	●	◐	◐	●	○	◐	○	○	●
Gourmet Mix	●	◐	◐	○	○	◐	○	○	●
Suet	●	○	○	○	●	●	○	○	○
Mealworms	●	○	○	○	○	○	○	○	●
Fresh Fruit	●	○	○	○	○	○	●	○	○
Dried Fruit	●	○	○	○	○	○	●	○	○
Grape Jelly	●	○	○	○	○	○	●	○	◐
Egg Shells	●	○	○	○	○	○	○	○	○
Peanut butter	●	○	○	○	●	○	○	○	○
Nectar	○	○	○	○	○	○	●	●	●

CHAPTER SIX

The Watering Hole

Every bird out in the wild needs water to survive. By adding water to your feeding station you increase the chances of any bird showing up. Birds need water not only for drinking, but also for bathing to keep feathers healthy. Birds that don't typically come to seed feeders, such as a Cedar Waxwing, robin or Brown Thrasher, love a good birdbath.

Brown Thrashers don't always come to bird feeders, but they will come to birdbaths.

Birdbaths can be as gorgeous and decorative as anything you could possibly imagine or as natural looking as a small pond—the possibilities are endless. Since many of them can look like a piece of art you can easily keep one on a deck or patio without causing too much trouble with an apartment manager or association. Keep in mind that it may take birds a while to figure out some of the more decorative baths are water sources. Think about it; in the wild, how often do you see a dish suspended in a tree for birds to drink out of? That's usually the reason why they don't notice that adorable hanging birdbath you just purchased.

Water for birds should be placed in the same general feeding area you've made for the birds, but avoid having water directly under feeders. Birds are messy eaters and birdbaths are tough enough to keep clean without added seeds and shells in the water.

Apartment Birder Tip

Birds don't need an Olympic-size pool to take a bath. A small tray with half an inch of water can attract a variety of birds. It helps call their attention to the tray if a dripping sound or feeder station is placed nearby.

Birds typically find water on the ground, so by placing your birdbath low you increase the chances that birds will find it. Birds also see water easier in darker colored baths as opposed to lighter colored birdbaths. If you can, try to have several levels in the bath. A Black-capped Chickadee is going to have an easier time in a shallower bath than a robin. For most birds, an inch and a half of water is plenty. If you have one deep birdbath try adding decorative rocks to give it more levels.

Birds also find baths by sound as opposed to sight. The sound of moving water really brings them in. There are several options for getting water to move in a basic birdbath.

Drippers

Dark-colored birdbaths usually attract visitors more quickly than lighter baths. Here, an Indigo Bunting is announcing its territory before freshening up.

This is a device that typically has an adapter so it can be attached to your garden hose. You can control the amount of water that flows through the tubes to be a trickle or just a steady drip. You don't have to run it twenty-four hours, seven days a week; just when you are home to enjoy the birds.

Misters

Some birds easily find baths, but you will attract even more guests by adding a dripper for noise. You can also use a mist to draw hummingbirds; watch them zip back and forth in the spray in order to "take a shower."

Misters are also attached to garden hoses with adapters and create a fine mist over your bath. Hummingbirds will be your primary guests at a mister.

Robins are eager bathers and are fun to watch.

Hummingbirds cannot walk; their legs are immobile. If they are sitting on a branch and want to face the opposite direction they must fly straight up, turn around in midair and then land. They prefer to get their water on the wing and are attracted by misting water. Hummingbirds also find sprinklers attractive; they'll zip back and forth in the spray.

Pumps

When water is scarce, resourceful birds like this Northern Mockingbird will seek it anywhere they can find it, including public drinking fountains.

Pumps are by far the easiest water-mover to add to a birdbath. They are either electrical or solar-powered and keep the water moving with a pleasant and relaxing sound. You do have to keep an eye on your pump, though. If the water evaporates and the pump runs dry, the life of the pump can be affected. Some are made to look like drippers, while others can spray straight up into the air or gently gurgle out of a fake rock.

Wigglers

Wigglers are fairly new and basically are battery powered motors that have arms to spin the water around. They are nice because they keep the water moving but don't use electricity. They also can keep running even if the birdbath is empty and not get damaged. They don't make much noise compared to a pump or dripper, but they are a nice addition to most baths.

Heated Birdbaths

Heated birdbaths are a great way to attract birds in the winter. If birds cannot find open water in winter they will eat snow to survive, which is hard on their metabolism, so many will welcome a quick drink from a bath. A heated bath is only warm enough to keep water open, not to keep the water warm, so it will not feel like a hot tub if you stick your finger in it on a cold day.

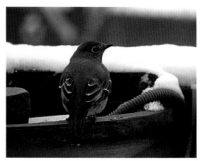

During winter, heated baths might attract Eastern Bluebirds and other surprising visitors.

Most heated birdbaths are electrical and use the equivalent of a 60-watt light bulb. There are a few solar-powered models, but most northern states do not get enough daylight in winter for them to work. Heated birdbaths are controlled by a thermostat and will shut off automatically when the temperature is around 40 degrees Fahrenheit.

If you already have a birdbath, you can add a heater to it. However, if the birdbath is terra cotta, concrete or cement, it does run the risk of cracking. On days when the temperature is below zero degrees Fahrenheit you will notice ice forming on the edges of the bath. If there are any minute cracks in the bath, water in the cracks will freeze as well, expanding the crack and breaking the bath over time. Always use a birdbath heater with a plastic dish.

There is some concern about birds bathing in winter and then freezing to death. On the rare occasion when birds bathe in winter it is usually a non-native species called the European Starling, which is overpopulated in North America and competes with our native species. Since the starling is non-native, I have to wonder if it is

When water isn't available, birds will eat snow for moisture. However, water helps them burn fewer calories than snow does.

not used to not bathing in winter and if that is the reason it tends to bathe in freezing temperatures. There is no scientific data to back that theory, just speculation on my part.

My opinion is that a bird that bathes in open water when it's below freezing has other problems going on. Open water will always be available near power plants along rivers. Birds should be smart enough not to bathe when it's dangerously cold. Rare occurrences of this behavior have been documented in Blue Jays, robins, goldfinches and at least one cardinal that I know of. It's rare to have trouble, but if it is something that you are concerned about, either don't offer open water in winter or place wooden slats over the top of the birdbath with only enough space for a bird to stick its head through, eliminating the temptation for it to bathe.

Keeping the Bath Clean

Birdbaths need to be kept clean, just like bird feeders. One tool is an enzyme solution called Birdbath Protector, which is 100 percent safe for birds to drink and consumes algae and sludge that can build up in a birdbath. Even using this product you will still have to periodically clean out the bath, especially if your tap water has lots of minerals in it. The best method is a wash with a mild solution of bleach and water. You can also let the bath soak overnight in straight white vinegar and the next day use old-fashioned elbow grease to scrub it with a good stiff brush.

With West Nile Virus, there's lots of concern about mosquitoes using a birdbath as a breeding ground. You can either dump the water out on a daily basis and refill it or add a dripper or wiggler to keep the water moving (mosquitoes won't lay eggs on moving water). Or you can use a product called Mosquito Free Water. It's an enzyme that you spray on top of the bath once a week. It breaks the surface tension of the water that a female mosquito needs in order to land and lay her eggs. Without the surface tension, when she lands, she sinks and dies. Regardless of mosquitoes you will need to keep the water fresh in your bath for the birds. The best thing is to change the water to keep it clean.

Even Cooper's Hawks need to keep their feathers clean and in good condition.

CHAPTER SEVEN

Shelter For Birds

Another way to provide for birds without using a bird feeder is to offer shelter, either in the form of a place to nest in warmer months or a roosting box in winter.

OPPOSITE: Black-capped Chickadee

Not all birds nest in houses. The most common birds that use nest boxes are:

House Wren
House Sparrow
Black-capped Chickadee
Tree Swallow
Purple Martin
Eastern Bluebird
European Starling
Wood Duck
Eastern Screech-Owl
American Kestrel

Gray phase Eastern Screech-Owl

Choosing a Good Bird House

Be sure when choosing a bird house to select a quality product. A good bird house will be put together with screws and nails, not glue. Glue can be dangerous as it can come apart after several rain storms.

Make sure the bird house is made out of a sturdy material such as cedar and is well ventilated. Ventilation holes are typically found at the top just under the roof of the bird house. They are small slits or holes to allow air flow, but not large enough to be used as an entrance.

Avoid purchasing a bird house with a perch; it is unnecessary and makes it more awkward for parents to feed their chicks. Plus it encourages predators to get in and eat the chicks or eggs by offering a foothold.

A good bird house should have a way of easily opening up so you can clean it out in the fall. Some bird species, such as Eastern Bluebirds, will reuse the same house in the summer if it is cleaned out as soon as their brood leaves the nest.

Setting Up Bird Houses

Bird houses do best when they are mounted on poles with a raccoon guard. Houses mounted on trees are at a high risk of predation by raccoons, squirrels, snakes, mink and weasels. Most bird houses can be mounted at least five feet high or near your eye level, even a Wood Duck box. Sure, some birds will nest as high as fifty feet up, but that's a pain for you when you have to clean the bird house out in the fall or if you need to do any kind of repairs to the bird house.

Some birds such as House Wrens will nest in a hanging house, but most birds prefer nesting boxes that are post mounted. I have had chickadees attempt to nest in a hanging house, but the house blew down in a wind storm and the eggs were lost. Again, it is much easier to keep a bird house secure and safe from predators if it is mounted to a post with a baffle.

A Peterson-style bluebird box works best in wide-open habitat.

Wood Duck boxes don't need to be fifty feet in the air. A box six feet high with a sturdy raccoon baffle will attract hen woodies and will be easier for you to maintain in the fall.

Monitoring Bird Houses

A clutch of Wood Duck eggs will hatch within twenty-four hours of each other.

It's a good idea to check what is going on inside the bird house once or twice a week. This will not cause the parent birds to abandon the nest (although it might cause them to swoop down at your head, so be sure to duck). This allows you to see what's going on; if a house needs a minor repair after a storm you can take care of it, if something has attacked the nest box, you can clean it out right away so that it could get used again. In early- to mid-summer if you clean out a nest as soon as the parent birds are finished raising a batch of chicks, the house might get used again.

Try to take a notebook with you and keep track of hatching dates. Many birds will be getting flight feathers at around thirteen days after hatching and it's not safe to check inside the nest box any more. When the chicks are thirteen days old, opening the box at that point puts them at a higher risk of leaving the nest box too soon. Once a feathered baby bird is out of the nest box, it's next to impossible to talk it into going back in. Once all the babies have left the nest box, it is safe to clean out and get ready for the next tenant.

When all of the ducklings hatch the hen will call to them, and they will leap into the water to join her. Incredibly, ducklings are capable of jumping from as high as 50 feet.

Check your bird houses once a week.

Bluebirds will become accustomed to your presence and, as in the case of this trusting female, may even stay put when you open the box.

Use some common sense when monitoring nests. I can't tell you the number of times I have almost lost an eye when checking nest boxes. When I was in college, my roommate Laura and I found a bird nest at eye level. I was curious about what eggs or chicks might be inside. I grabbed Laura and made a bee line for the nest. Not being into birds at all or just having way more common sense than me, Laura released herself from my grasp and kept her distance. I peered inside and found four naked chicks and exclaimed, "Oh, Laura, you should see this." I heard Laura cautiously say, "Uh, Sharon . . . " and before I knew it, I had a face full of feathers. Apparently it was a robin nest and the male was very effective at keeping dorks like me from getting too close. I had a scratch an inch away from my left eyeball for a few days. I was lucky it wasn't worse.

You would think that incident taught me a lesson, but I almost lost my eye to a House Wren by keeping my eye at the nest box entrance hole as I opened the side. Mental note: Always keep your eyeball away from the entrance of nest box holes. When you open the nest box, you will find out soon enough what is inside.

Nest Box Users

The type of bird you get using a nest box depends on the size of the box, the size of the entrance hole and the type of habitat in which the bird house is located. Some birds are controversial and it will be up to you as to whether or not you wish them to nest in your habitat.

Brown-headed Cowbirds

Some people will look in a nest and notice that there is an egg that is different from the other eggs: these are usually Brown-headed Cowbird eggs. The Brown-headed Cowbird is an unusual species when it comes to nesting. They evolved to follow herds of buffalo across the plains. The buffalo would kick up insects in their travels and the cowbirds would feed on them. This is not an ideal lifestyle for raising chicks. Buffalo herds move and the cowbirds had to follow the food supply. So, cowbirds evolved to deposit their eggs in other species' nests. This worked out well as the cowbirds moved around; not too many species were negatively affected.

One of these things is not like the others. The larger egg is from a cowbird.

Then something changed. The massive herds of buffalo disappeared and cowbirds started following humans instead. Humans don't travel as much as a buffalo herd so cowbirds spend the summers in a neighborhood. One female cowbird in a neighborhood is capable of laying dozens of eggs causing problems especially for species such as warblers and thrushes.

Some species have evolved to avoid problems with cowbird chicks in the nest. For example, goldfinches feed their chicks more seeds than insects and a young cowbird needs an insect heavy diet. Cowbird chicks do not survive well in goldfinch nests. Other birds such as Common Yellowthroats feed lots of insects and sometimes you will see a tiny adult bird feeding a begging chick that is four times its size.

A soon-to-fledge cowbird

If you find a Brown-headed Cowbird egg in a bird nest, you are faced with a choice. Do you remove the cowbird egg or let Nature take its course? According to the Migratory Bird Treaty Act, it is technically illegal to remove a cowbird egg, since it is a native North American bird, unlike House Sparrows and European Starlings. It's entirely up to you whether or not to remove the egg. In some places, such as the breeding grounds of the rare and endangered Kirtland's Warbler, cowbirds and their eggs are legally removed with a depredation permit to keep cowbirds from disrupting the nesting practices of this dwindling species. Will your removal of one cowbird egg from a House Finch nest make a difference? Probably not in the grand scheme of this bird's population, but maybe to the nest that is right in front of you. However, the removal of cowbird eggs is illegal.

Killdeer do not use nest boxes. Instead these ground nesters are often found in yards, especially on gravel.

Apartment Birder Tip

If your apartment is on or near the ground floor, you have a good chance of attracting nesting wrens and chickadees. Higher apartments are more likely to attract House Finches and Tree Swallows.

The Migratory Bird Treaty Act of 1918

The Migratory Bird Treaty was set up for the protection of native birds in North America. It essentially says that it is illegal to hunt, take, capture, kill or sell any native migratory bird or to have any parts of a migratory bird including feathers, nests, eggs or anything without state and federal permits.

The laws are in place primarily to go after poachers. If a person is suspected of, say, poaching woodpeckers and someone from the U.S. Fish and Wildlife Service tries to prosecute them, it's hard to prove poaching unless they catch someone in the act of killing the woodpecker. So, when someone has a whole bunch of woodpecker feathers and the U.S. Fish and Wildlife Service suspects poaching, if the suspected poacher says, "Hey, I just found these feathers in the woods, I didn't poach them," the law is in place to say, "Well, you don't have a permit for those feathers so you'll need to be fined for having them in your possession."

Let's make one thing clear: the law is mostly used when poaching is suspected, otherwise the U.S. Fish and Wildlife Service would be hauling in second-graders across the country by the thousands since kids love to pick up feathers. However, according to the law, the feathers—even feathers that have been molted out—should be left outside. It's also a good idea to leave feathers outside since there are creatures, such as Tree Swallows, that will use discarded feathers to line their nests.

The law also applies when it comes to pests in the yard. If a House Wren is poking holes in all your bluebird eggs, killing the wrens is a violation and if you are caught, you could be fined since wrens are a native species. Unlike House Sparrows, House Wrens were not introduced to North America, but evolved along with Eastern Bluebirds. It could be argued that bluebirds need to learn to defend the nest from wrens without our intervention. House Sparrows are a recent addition to the North American ecosystem that bluebirds haven't had time to develop a defense against so our intervention could be helpful when it comes to House Sparrows.

One-Inch Hole

A Wood Duck box inhabited by a House Wren and its characteristic nest full of sticks.

House Wren eggs

These House Wren chicks are almost ready to leave the nest.

Small houses with a one-inch hole will only get House Wrens, because it is the smallest bird that will use a nest cavity in North America. House Wrens are boisterous little singers that eat tons of insects. They tend to nest near brushy areas but can be found on the edges of woodlands and will nest in fields. For such tiny birds, they are incredibly industrious, with males building five to six nests from which the female chooses. After she has chosen the nest for the brood, the male will still defend all the nests, using the empty ones as decoys to fool predators.

House Wrens are tiny, but they're boisterous singers that eat plenty of insects.

Wrens can be fun birds, but for people who have bluebird houses up, House Wrens can sometimes cause problems. If a pair of wrens wants to use a nest box badly enough they will sometimes poke holes in the bluebird eggs so they won't hatch and then take over the nest box when the bluebirds abandon it. House Wrens are native to North America and their nests and eggs are protected under the Migratory Bird Treaty Act.

House Wrens will nest in just about anything, including old shoes, unused mailboxes, pockets of jackets left sitting outside too long or anything else they can put sticks into. They do not seem to have a preference of whether a bird house is hanging or post mounted and will nest anywhere from four feet to twenty feet high.

House Wren nests are easily identifiable by the massive amount of sticks tossed in an apparent hodgepodge fashion inside the nest box. Their eggs are tan with brown marks.

Inch-and-an-Eighth Hole

House Wrens will nest anywhere from three to ten feet high.

Birds tend to have an easier time using nest boxes without perches.

Small houses with a hole size of an inch and an eighth will get House Wrens or chickadees, either Carolina or Black-capped. Chickadees seem to prefer a post-mounted house, but will still use a hanging bird house. Chickadees can typically nest compatibly with Eastern Bluebirds or Tree Swallows.

Chickadees will nest anywhere from three feet to twenty feet high and tend to nest on the edges of woodlands or in the woods. The nest is easily identifiable as a neat cup made of moss and grasses, usually lined with fur. Chickadee eggs are white with fine brownish markings.

Inch-and-a-Quarter Hole

This is an entrance hole that could accommodate House Sparrows, chickadees or House Wrens. If a House Sparrow is in the neighborhood it will generally try to take over the box and not allow anyone else to nest in there. House Sparrows will either nest on their own or several House Sparrows can take over a colony-style house such as a Purple Martin house.

House Sparrows can wreak havoc on other cavity-nest species by driving them away from nest boxes.

House Sparrows are on the controversial side when it comes to attracting birds. They were introduced to the United States in the 1850s and have been very successful here. Because they are not considered a native species they are not protected under the Migratory Bird Treaty Act and removal of House Sparrow nests, eggs, nestlings and the House Sparrows themselves is perfectly legal. However, it is often easier said than done.

Like House Wrens, House Sparrows get aggressive when they decide they want a nest box. House Sparrows will go in and kill anything in the box in order to take it over, and that includes eggs, chicks and even adult birds. House Sparrows have a large and thick bill and they can use it to peck the skulls of other birds. Many wonder why people dislike House Sparrows so much, but if you ever come across a bluebird or chickadee nest that has been hit by a House Sparrow, you can begin to understand the anger surrounding this bird. The House Sparrows will build their nest right on top of the destroyed eggs or the carcasses of nestlings or adult birds.

House Sparrows will nest anywhere they possibly can. Their nests are easily identifiable by the packrat look of the nest. You will find just about everything but the kitchen sink in a House Sparrow nest: grasses, feathers, cellophane, cigarette butts and paper. House Sparrow eggs are white with brown markings.

Inch-and-Three-Quarters Hole

| Gilwood-style bluebird box | Peterson-style bluebird box | Gilbertson-style bluebird box |

Medium-sized houses with this size entrance hole are often referred to as bluebird boxes because that is the intended occupant, but you can get Tree Swallows, chickadees, House Wrens or House Sparrows using the boxes.

Bluebirds and Tree Swallows tend to occupy open fields or the edges of woodlands. Because they are larger birds, the hole needs to be larger, but that means every other smaller bird out there that uses nest boxes

Tree Swallows will share territory with Eastern Bluebirds and will help defend the nest boxes from predators.

might want to nest in the box. Because of this, bluebird boxes usually do best when mounted in pairs with the two houses within ten feet of each other. Pairs of houses are then mounted every three hundred feet. Bluebirds can take one box, and then a chickadee or Tree Swallow will take the other and they can defend the territory together. If a House Sparrow or House Wren takes over one of the boxes it's highly unlikely they will allow a bluebird to nest in the other box in the pair. Unfortunately, there is no good way to discourage wrens and sparrows from using these boxes.

Bluebirds and Tree Swallows are becoming more tolerant of humans and their nest boxes can be found in city parks or golf courses provided that there are enough insects for them to eat. When monitoring a bluebird box, many people will take live mealworms and either leave them on the roof of the bluebird box or in a cup attached to the pole on the house. By leaving the mealworms when you visit, the adult bluebirds will see you as a bonus instead of a pain when you stop by. Since meal-worms aren't a favorite food of squirrels and raccoons, you won't have to worry about drawing preda-tors too close to the boxes.

Mealworm feeders can be placed on bluebird boxes. To put the bluebirds at ease, offer meal-worms whenever you check your nest boxes.

Bluebird nests are a neat cup of grasses with softer fibers in the center. Their eggs are pale blue. Tree Swallow nests will look similar but the inside of the nest cup will be lined with feathers, preferably white, but any color will do in a pinch. They gather feathers that they find on the ground and for some reason seem to prefer white feathers from domestic ducks and geese. Tree Swallow eggs are plain white.

Tree Swallow eggs are often surrounded by feathers.

Bluebird chicks. Note the lack of feathers in the nest.

Apartment Birder Tip

If there is a pond or lake in the neighborhood, talk to the building manager about the possibility of adding Wood Duck nest boxes. They can be a fun addition to the property.

Big Houses

Large houses with oval holes can get Wood Ducks, starlings, American Kestrels and Eastern Screech-Owls. Once the house is occupied, it's not

as essential to check on them as often as you do chickadee and bluebird boxes. The birds that use them tend to be more skittish anyway and disturbing the females too much during incubation could cause them to abandon the nest.

After mating, the male Wood Duck leaves the female to incubate the eggs and to rear the young on her own.

Small falcons called American Kestrels will sometimes use a Wood Duck box, too.

This box includes a screen for climbing.

This screen helps the young enter the box.

Wood Ducks will fly right into the box at lightning fast speed.

This box for Wood Ducks or Hooded Mergansers can be mounted so that the bottom of the box is as low as six feet. The box should have a layer of cedar bedding or shavings on the bottom for the Wood Duck. Wood Ducks and mergansers will nest in metro areas within a half-mile of lakes, ponds or streams. The female will lay eggs and line the cedar chips with down from her breast. She will incubate the eggs for about thirty days and all the chicks will hatch at the same time. Within a day of hatching all the chicks crawl up to the nest box hole and jump down to the ground below, joining the female as she takes them into the water to safety and food. As soon as they are gone it is safe to clean out the house. Wood Duck and merganser boxes generally only get used once in a summer.

One thing you can do with ducks in a box is stick a digital camera in and take a photo once or twice a week. If you are quick about it, it doesn't disturb the incubating female too much and you can get some fun photos out of it.

Other birds that can show up in these types of boxes include star-

This Wood Duck chick leaves the nest box, just 24 hours after hatching.

Sometimes other waterfowl, such as Hooded Mergansers, will nest in your Wood Duck box.

lings, which are also an introduced species. They have blue eggs with brown markings and will fill the nest box with all kinds of stuff, but tend to avoid nesting low, so will usually avoid the house if it is mounted only six feet up.

Raptors such as Eastern Screech-Owls or American Kestrels will use a box like this, but generally prefer the box to be twenty to fifty feet in the air and without cedar bedding inside. I don't think you have to be as high as twenty feet. My sister, Robin, has never been a birder and when she and her husband bought their dream home a few years ago, it came with an old wooden Purple Martin nest box. The box looked as though it had been up at least ten years and some of the holes had been chewed wider by squirrels. It was mounted about fourteen feet high. One day Robin called and told me about a bird that was hanging around the house but didn't look anything like a Purple Martin. The bird was about the size of a Blue Jay and was orange and blue with a line under each eye—it was a male American Kestrel, and he soon wooed in a female. The holes were wide enough to allow the small falcons inside and they nested in there that spring. Robin is now quite the backyard birder thanks to those guys. And again, that is an example of not the best housing in the world and certainly not textbook housing but good enough for that particular pair of kestrels.

Eastern Screech-Owls and American Kestrels are common in metro and suburban areas. We had a pair of red Screech-Owls nest a few blocks from our apartment in Minneapolis. They nested in a wood-pecker hole in a tree about twenty feet up. I have also seen them in old Wood Duck boxes that aren't more than ten feet off the ground. I'm sure the screeches would prefer a higher box, but if there are not a lot of options, this adaptable species will make do with whatever nest box is available.

Eastern Screech-Owl (red morph) that nested a few blocks from my apartment.

Purple Martins

Ah, Purple Martins, in some areas so easy to attract, in others so seemingly out of reach. Purple martins are the largest swallow in North America. Depending on who you talk to, they are loyal tenants and delightful song-sters who spend their day snarfing up mosquitoes on the wing. Or, they are high maintenance and noisy birds that ignore your expensive and properly placed housing year after year after year.

Purple Martins are colony nesters and originally used dead trees full of wood-pecker holes as nesting cavities. Over the years, this species adapted to using man made housing including elaborate houses and gourds. Good quality martin houses can be made of aluminum, wood, or thick plastic. Many ex-perienced purple martin landlords will have differ-ent (and strong) opinions as to what is best for the Purple Martin. Housing should be white, to help

Purple Martins are hard to attract, but they are loyal tenants once you get their attention. Purple Martins are communal nesters, meaning they like to nest in large groups. You must provide at least four compartments to qualify as a martin house.

keep the interior cool in high temperatures and in general should be twelve to twenty feet high on a telescoping pole so that you can lower the house once a week and monitor what is going on inside the colony.

The biggest mistake people make when installing purple martin houses is placement. Martins like to perch high to be able to watch the surrounding area for aerial bugs and predators. Houses are most successful when placed 40 to 60 feet away from trees or buildings and near water. It also helps if the house is within 100 feet of human habitation.

Male Purple Martin

Once you have the housing up, you need to be proactive to keep House Sparrows and European Starlings out. Some people keep the entrance holes plugged up until martins appear in the area, and then gradually open the housing up. If sparrows and starlings start nesting in the box, martins will avoid it.

If you are thinking of adding a martin house to your yard, do some research and find out if there is a Purple Martin Club or at least someone nearby with experience attracting martins who might give you some tips for the area. For example, if there is someone in and around your neighborhood who has had success attracting martins with plastic gourds, it might be easier for you to start with that, since the martins in the area are used to looking for that shape for nesting.

On a final note, monitoring your Purple Martin colony will help insure nesting success. Like managing a bluebird trail, weekly checks of a martin colony can be educational, fun, and help you detect and stop problems like snakes sneaking into the nests. Some purple martin landlords will go so far as to advise visiting the nest colony every day and to change out the nesting material with fresh nesting material every day to ensure healthy chicks.

It's one thing to help a wild species by building housing that is no longer available naturally. However, doing something to a nest that is not something the birds would do anyway, is going too far. Martins would not normally rebuild a nest every day, and if you are doing this for them, that is not helping a species to survive in the wild, that is closer to treating a Purple Martin like a pet.

Female Purple Martin

Holey Nestboxes Batman

MOST LIKELY TO WORK ●
KINDA' LIKELY TO WORK ◐
HIGHLY UNLIKELY TO WORK ○

	1" hole	1⅛" hole	1¼" hole	1¾" hole	4"x3" oval	nesting ledge/shelf
Bluebird, Eastern	○	○	○	●	○	○
Chickadee, Black-capped	○	◐	◐	◐	◐	○
Chickadee, Carolina	○	◐	◐	◐	◐	○
Dove, Mourning	○	○	○	○	○	●
Duck, Wood	○	○	○	○	●	○
Finch, House	○	○	○	○	○	●
Kestrel, American	○	○	○	○	●	○
Martin, Purple	○	○	○	●	○	○
Merganser, Hooded	○	○	○	○	●	○
Phoebe, Eastern	○	○	○	○	○	●
Robin, American	○	○	○	○	○	●
Screech-Owl, Eastern	○	○	○	○	●	○
Sparrow, House	○	○	◐	◐	◐	○
Starling, European	○	○	○	○	●	○
Swallow, Barn	○	○	○	○	○	●
Swallow, Tree	○	○	○	◐	◐	○
Titmouse, Tufted	○	○	◐	◐	◐	◐
Wren, House	◐	◐	◐	◐	◐	○

Alternative Housing

Not all birds that nest on or near our homes use nest boxes. House Finches love to nest in unusual places. They are fond of hanging plant baskets, decorative wreaths and climbing vines. If a nest box is not an option for you, try decorating outside your windows and decks with these things to see if anything nests there. After all, it's not your fault that you had a beautiful spring wreath on your door and a robin or House Finch decided to move in and raise a family.

This House Finch nest is tucked inside a hanging flower basket.

You can purchase or make nesting shelves. These are little ledges that can be left in their natural state or painted to match the decorations on your deck. Many birds can use these, including House Finches, Barn Swallows, robins, Mourning Doves and Eastern Phoebes. They seem to work best when mounted just under an eave or above a window.

Roosting boxes are a relatively new addition to backyards. There are different types, such as a large chickadee roosting box. The box is large and the entrance hole is at the bottom of the box. Chickadees enter to find several perches and wire mesh on the sides of the box. The theory is that winter flocks of chickadees will fly inside and roost together for warmth in the winter. Personally, I have not had much success with a roosting box, but I have met people who have had them work—as evidenced by the little chickadee poops found at the entrance hole. The boxes tend to be used by birds when placed near a feeding station or mounted to the side of a conifer. Since the hole is at the bottom of the box and the box is so large, predators tend to leave it alone.

Grass nesting huts are available for birds to roost in as well. They are a bit more decorative than a traditional roosting box, but I'm not

These House Finch chicks hatch in a nest that was built in a cement cup meant for Barn Swallows.

sure how effective they are for attracting birds. I think these pouches work best in the southern half of the United States where the winters are milder. Pouches are typically sold in pet stores for domestic finches to use for nesting. Somehow they crossed over to the wild bird industry and popped up everywhere. Apart from House Sparrows, I don't know of any other North American bird species that would use them. They won't keep moisture out, so they wouldn't be ideal for nesting for chickadees or house wrens. I have seen photos of House Finches using them for nesting and of Carolina Wrens using them for roosting or nesting.

Apartment Birder Tip

Sometimes the subtle approach works best. For example, a hanging plant basket is an open invitation for nesting House Finches to join the neighborhood.

Nesting Material

You can offer nesting materials to birds in an artistic fashion.

In the spring and summer birds are on the lookout for nesting material. One of my favorite things to put out is raw cotton. One spring I put out a ball and had Black-capped Chickadees, House Finches, Baltimore Orioles, Cedar Waxwings and American Goldfinches use it. You can also put out pet hair, human hair, yarn and string. If you put out yarn and string make sure that you keep the length short. Anything over six inches is a risk for birds to become tangled with the material.

There is some debate about whether or not dryer lint is safe for bird nesting material. Arguments have been made that the material could shrink if it gets wet, that it holds on to moisture for a long time, thus increasing the risk of hypothermia to the chicks in the nest, or that residual chemicals from laundry detergent or fabric softener could be harmful to the chicks. There is no scientific evidence to support that theory but I would advise erring on the side of caution by not using dryer lint. There are lots of other materials for birds to use to build a nest.

This Eastern Kingbird nest is lined with string that is dangerously long. Young birds learning to fly could get tangled and never leave the nest.

String cut 6 inches or less is safest for birds to use as nesting material. If you're going to put out string or yarn, make sure it's not longer than six inches.

Calling Cards

In the spring, male birds typically arrive first to try and set up a territory before prospective females arrive. Cavity-nesting birds will place a type of calling card inside the hole they have chosen. By monitoring your bird houses, you can get an idea about what species of male has booked your houses for his territory. Certainly, it's not an exact science, but most of the time it's right.

Male bluebirds will put in a fine piece of grass. Chickadees will typically put in a small bit of fur or moss. House Wrens will lay down a small twig and tree swallows will set in a feather. House Sparrows will drop in just about anything from cellophane to cigarette butts.

Wren calling card

The male will sing a song in his territory announcing, "All ladies come check me out, I'm the strongest and can provide the best food. I will give you lots of healthy eggs. All males, stay out!" A potential female will arrive and inspect the nest box. If she likes what she sees she will pick up the calling card and pair bonding will commence. If the house or territory is not to her liking, she will leave immediately and allow the male to continue his song.

Squatters! Nesting Where They're Not Wanted

Sometimes birds will pick a spot on or near your home that is just not a good idea, such as on a light fixtures, right over the front door or in a mailbox. If this happens, you need to take action right away for a couple of reasons. First, according to the Migratory Bird Treaty Act, you can't remove a nest of a native bird once it holds eggs or chicks. Second, birds are tenacious: if they see a spot they like and are successful raising a batch of chicks, they are going to do it again. Birds work fast,

You have a nook, house sparrows will turn it into a nest.

too. Think about it: build a nest in two or three days, incubate for twelve to sixteen days, feed the chicks in the nest for about twelve to thirteen days and they are off. In the grand scheme of a busy life, that is fast. So, as soon as you notice a bird nesting where you don't want it to nest, act fast. If the nest fails right away before eggs are even laid, that helps bring home the idea to the birds that this is not a good place to nest. Sometimes, especially in the case of Barn Swallows who make mud nests on your wall, you will

Mallards will sometimes choose to nest in flower beds near homes as a disguise from predators.

have to tear down the nests on a daily basis for several days. Stick with it, and the birds will get the idea that they are not wanted and eventually move on.

If a bird nests on your porch and you are afraid of using the porch for fear of scaring off the bird, don't worry. The bird has made what I call an informed decision. It watched the area for a few days before making the nest, noticed

Barn Swallows at a parking garage of a downtown mall.

Once swallows have successfully raised chicks it's almost impossible to deter them in the future.

the amount of human traffic and thought, "Yes, I can deal with this and raise a few chicks." I think sometimes birds choose a heavily people-trafficked area because predators avoid people.

C H A P T E R   E I G H T

Top Ten Most Wanted Guests

This section covers birds that most people want to attract. Some tips are included for attracting each species, but remember that the habitat has to be correct for the bird; if you're out of that bird's habitat, no amount of cajoling or pleading will bring that bird to your yard.

OPPOSITE: Eastern Bluebird

Northern Cardinal

Male Northern Cardinal

I've yet to meet the person who does not enjoy seeing cardinals. This bird is so popular that seven states have chosen it for their state bird.

Cardinals have an interesting habit of visiting feeders right at dawn and right at dusk, but can be found at anytime of day. During the breeding season you may only get one or two at a time, but in the winter they form large flocks and many people enjoy getting flocks of anywhere from six to forty birds.

Cardinals don't like other birds at the feeder while they are eating, and will often drive off smaller birds until they are finished. In mating season, watch for the male to feed the female as he would a young bird.

Another interesting thing to watch for is molting. In late summer and early fall many birds shed their old feathers and grow in fresh, strong ones for the winter. Birds with crested heads, such as Northern Cardinals or Blue Jays, will sometimes lose all their head feathers at once. Cardinals in particular look very strange because their skin is black and without their head feathers, their heads look tiny, especially compared to their fat bill. This is a normal part of the molting process and

Cardinal nests tend to be built low to the ground.

nothing to worry about. If the head is bare any other time of year, the bird may be suffering from feather mites. If you are able to catch the bird you can get it to a professional wildlife rehabilitator, but most strong, well-fed birds can survive a feather mite infestation, and healthy a bird will be too fast for you to catch.

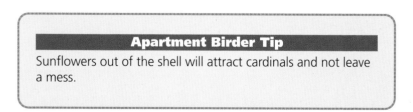

Apartment Birder Tip

Sunflowers out of the shell will attract cardinals and not leave a mess.

Attracting cardinals

Cardinals' favorite food is black-oil sunflower; however, they will also eat striped sunflower. Their large bills are ideal for cracking open hard-shelled seeds, but they have no problem eating hulled sunflower, too. Cardinals will also eat safflower, peanuts out of the shell and white millet. You can offer them non-traditional foods such as mealworms and fruit (cardinals appear to be particularly fond of pomegranates).

Juvenile (left) and female (right) Northern Cardinal

Female eating peanuts

Cardinals prefer yards that offer lots of cover for them to hide in before they visit the feeder. They are typically ground-feeding birds, but can be coaxed to feeding on second and third floors of buildings, provided that the perching area is large enough for them. Most tube feeders are designed for a bird to perch and turn to the side to feed out of the ports. This is usually not a problem for smaller chickadees and finches but cardinals have a tough time with this. If you want cardinals, make sure that the feeder has either a tray or some type of platform for the cardinal to fit its larger body on.

Don't bother trying to find a nest box for cardinals, they won't use one. Cardinals make cup nests fairly low to the ground in heavy cover. I've had them nest in a thick tangle of honeysuckle vines and in a huge brush pile. On occasion they will use a hanging plant basket, but that is not very common.

Black-capped and Carolina Chickadees

Black-capped and Carolina Chick-adees look almost identical.

Chickadees (either Black-capped or Carolina) are a welcome sight at the bird feeder. They can be found year-round in our yards and are just as fond of seeds as they are of insects. Cautious by nature, these birds will visit a feeder, take a sunflower seed and fly away to another perch to peck open the shell and eat the nutmeat on the inside. Even if you feed sunflower chips, these birds will grab the chip and fly to another perch to devour it.

In the winter, these birds will form what are called mixed flocks with nuthatches, titmice and Downy Woodpeckers. Being in a large group makes it easier to find food sources and means that there are more eyes to watch for potential predators.

Chickadees love mealworms.

Attracting chickadees

Aside from black-oil sunflower and sunflower chips, chickadees are also fond of safflower, peanuts, mixed nuts, Nyjer, pumpkin seeds and suet. Chickadees seem to have a knack for defying gravity and will use almost any type of feeder out there. As I type this, I realize that I have seen a chickadee on every style of feeder except a nectar feeder for hummingbirds. Wow.

Chickadees will gladly nest in a backyard and need a nest box with an entrance hole of at least an inch and an eighth in diameter. An entrance hole that small allows for the chickadee (but also the House Wren) and deters the House Sparrow. Chickadees prefer to nest in a post-mounted house, but occasionally nest in a hanging bird house.

Though they do not nest in winter, you can provide for them by putting up a roosting box. These boxes have one hole at the bottom of the box and multiple perches on the inside to allow for several birds to sleep.

Chickadees are quick to hand tame.

Baltimore Oriole

Male Baltimore Oriole

Female Balitmore Oriole

Orioles are a delight. Males are a vibrant orange and black and look almost too tropical for the Midwest. Orioles have a sweet beak as soon as they arrive and will eat copious amounts of jelly and nectar for the first month after arrival and then many people notice that they seem to disappear. Once chicks begin to hatch orioles switch to an insect-heavy diet. If you have orioles nesting in your yard, it is possible to see them all summer; if they are not nesting in your yard, they will seem to disappear once the chicks hatch. After the young leave the nest, the adults will bring them to grape jelly and nectar feeders and teach them how to feed out of them. You might also get a small influx of orioles right before they migrate south.

Attracting orioles

Orioles are an exciting bird to attract and can be tempted to your feeding station by providing nectar, orange halves or grape jelly. It is essential to keep the feeder clean. Think about it, would you want to eat grape jelly or oranges if they had been sitting outside for a week? The orioles don't like to either. If you would like to try to convince them to stick around once the chicks hatch, start adding mealworms to your jelly when they start to slow down at the feeder. They will welcome the extra protein source.

Orioles make pendulous nests.

Orioles make really cool-looking pendulous nests bags on the outer branches of trees such as willows and cotton-woods; they will not use a nest box. You can put out nesting material for them, such as six-inch pieces of yarn and raw cotton.

Ruby-throated Hummingbird

Male Ruby-throated Hummingbird

Hummingbirds are a delight in any yard. The first time my mother and I put up a feeder we had no success whatsoever. No one told us how important it was to clean out the feeder. I think we changed the nectar twice that summer and couldn't figure out why birds kept feeding on our Impatiens that bordered the sidewalk instead of partaking of the glorious red feeder right above.

I find that if you are in a metro area you may get one or two hummingbirds as opposed to more rural areas where you can have twenty coming at a time. Hummingbirds are very territorial and aggressive. After male and female hummingbirds mate, the female will drive the male out of her territory and raise the chicks on her own.

Hummingbirds not only rely on nectar for food, but eat a steady supply of tiny insects, which makes me wonder if the reason we don't see more hummingbirds in the metro areas has to do with pesticides. If we spray to keep insects away, that is taking away a vital part of the hummingbirds' diet and they will move elsewhere to find food.

Apartment Birder Tip

If your window or deck lacks color, tie a red ribbon or a few bright-red artificial flowers near nectar feeders to get the attention of hummingbirds and orioles. Avoid dripper style feeders. They will eave a sticky mess or ant moat.

Attracting hummingbirds

After mating, female hummingbirds drive males out of their territory and raise the chicks on their own.

Since hummingbirds are so territorial, sometimes a single hummingbird will take over the feeder and chase away any other hummer that tries to use it. If this happens, consider putting up a second feeder in your yard. Having a hummingbird feeder in the front yard and the backyard works very well. If the two feeders are within twenty feet of the other, it is possible for one hummingbird to try to defend both feeders, so keeping them a good distance apart is essential. If you are in a rural area where there are plenty of insects for hummingbirds, this is rarely a problem; in those types of areas you can get several hummingbirds feeding at once.

It is imperative to clean the hummingbird feeder often. If you had a soda outside, how many days would go by before you wouldn't want to drink it? Hummingbirds feel the same way. At the very least, a nectar feeder should be cleaned every two days if it is in direct sun or every five days if it is in the shade. If you ever find any slime or fungus inside the feeder, make sure to wash it out with antibacterial soap and rinse it thoroughly before putting it back outside.

If you are reading this and thinking, "I can barely manage to do the dishes once a week. How the heck am I going to keep a hummingbird feeder clean?" you might consider using plants to attract hummingbirds instead. Hummingbirds are attracted to nectar-rich flowers such as cardinal climber, impatiens, honeysuckle, trumpet vine, columbine, foxglove, bee balm, delphinium, coneflower and salvia.

Female Ruby-throated Hummingbird

Rose-breasted Grosbeak

Male Rose-breasted Grosbeak

During the spring migration, before insects are out in full force, many people are delighted to see this colorful bird at the feeder. Rose-breasted Grosbeaks announce their arrival in spring by sounding like a robin that has taken opera lessons and by their chip note that sounds like a sneaker squeaking on a gym floor.

Rose-breasted Grosbeaks are about the size of a Northern Cardinal, and the males are very classy looking with their black backs, white bellies and oh-so-tasteful splash of pink on the chest. The female is white with brown streaking, strongly resembling a larger version of a female Purple Finch.

Attracting grosbeaks

Female Rose-breasted Grosbeak

These birds have the same tastes as cardinals and also prefer feeders with large perching areas. Though these birds eat sunflower, I find that they seem to prefer safflower over any other feed. Rose-breasteds will come in for dried fruit and mealworms as well, but once the weather heats up and insects are out in full force, grosbeaks will ignore feeders and become natural insect exterminators in your neighborhood.

Rose-breasted Grosbeaks will not use a nest box, so your best bet is to try to lure them in with a bird feeder.

Pileated Woodpecker

Male Pileated Woodpecker

There are oodles of woodpeckers for people to attract, but this is the one that always gets attention. This particular bird is in dire need of a name change to something more along the lines of the HUGE woodpecker.

The name can be pronounced either Pie-lee-ated or Pill-e-ated and on rare occasions I have heard it referred to has the Pee-lee-ated or even the pleated woodpecker. Whatever you want to call it, it's huge and you won't mistake it for any other bird in your yard.

It always seems to me that the larger a bird is, the more skittish it is around humans. The Pileated Woodpecker is known to be timid, but it's learning to overcome that and visit suet and peanut feeders all over the eastern half of the United States

Sometimes they try to feed on the small cage suet feeders, but usually have such a tough time that they give up rather quickly. If you have seen these birds in your neighborhood, it's well worth your while to invest in a long suet log or double cake suet feeder or even try to find a way to secure a large suet feeder to the trunk of a tree. It's a big woodpecker with a big appetite and thus needs a large feeder.

Female Pileated Woodpecker

Attracting woodpeckers

Peanuts and suet seem to be the way to the Pileated Woodpecker's heart. Offer both in holders that are large enough to accommodate the size of this woodpecker. I find that suet logs or cage style feeders with a wooden paddle on the bottom for tail support work best. Though woodpeckers are cavity nesters, it is rare for one to use a nest box. I think they prefer to do it themselves. You can help provide nesting habitat by leaving up dead or dying trees for as long as possible, since they are woodpeckers' preferred nest spots. I know some people who find dead tree trunks and then "install" them into their yard with cement. They cut off any branches that might fall and leave the rest up for woodpeckers. Your human neighbors will think you are odd as ducks, but your woodpecker neighbors will love you for it.

Eastern Bluebird

A female bluebird teaches its young to feed.

Eastern Bluebirds are slightly smaller than American Robins. Males are sky blue on the back with an orange breast. Females are similar in color, but lack the brilliant blue coloring on the head and shoulders. Typically, bluebirds are not seed eaters, but prefer insects and berries. In extreme cold temperatures, bluebirds have been known to visit tray feeders for sunflower chips and suet but their primary interest is insects.

These birds are little bit higher maintenance, but well worth the effort. Many people think that bluebirds are only possible in the remote countryside, but in Minneapolis there is a city park with a small population of Eastern Bluebirds.

Attracting bluebirds

Since bluebirds aren't primarily seed eaters, they usually don't visit bird feeders as they don't recognize a feeder as source of food, even if you offer mealworms. You have to kind of train them into using feeders. The key to getting bluebirds to hang around is bluebird house maintenance. After you have bluebirds established in the house, you can mount a small cup to the pole and deposit mealworms in there. Once bluebirds recognize the cup as a source of food, you can move the cup closer and closer to your feeders until bluebirds figure out the food source. I know of some customers who get bluebirds feeding off of suction cup window feeders.

Make sure your bluebird houses are properly mounted. Bluebird houses should be pole-mounted in pairs, each house within ten feet of the other.

Pairs should then be mounted three hundred feet apart. Bluebirds are a large bird, so they need an entrance hole that is at least an inch and three quarters. Because of this, several species of birds will use a bluebird house, including chickadees, House Wrens, Tree Swallows and House Sparrows. The bluebird appears to be the least aggressive of all the species so even if a bluebird already has a house staked out, it is possible for a Tree Swallow to drive the bluebird away. By having the houses mounted in pairs, the bluebird can take one and the Tree Swallows will take the other and they will defend the territory together.

I can't stress the importance of checking bird houses at least once a week. It is a fun family activity and if something goes wrong in the nest box, you can immediately clean it out, making it possible for the birds to renest.

Male Eastern Bluebird

American Goldfinch

Male goldfinch

I find goldfinches to be a little finicky and I wonder if the males are so pretty they know they can get away with it! Goldfinch males are a gorgeous yellow in summer and a dull olive in winter. Because of this plumage change, many assume the goldfinch migrates, but it can be attracted to feeders year-round. In the summer goldfinches will stay in one territory; in the fall they form large nomadic flocks of up to hundreds of birds. One week you will be inundated with them, the next week they will leave, only to return two weeks later. This is very normal as they travel the area in search of food.

Attracting goldfinches

Goldfinches can be picky about the quality of their seed. For example, if your Nyjer seed is over six months old or has gotten wet, the birds will not eat it. Purchase Nyjer often, in small quantities, to ensure that it stays fresh.

Goldfinches will not use a nest box, but will come in for cotton nesting material. I usually hang mine within a few feet of my finch feeder. You don't have worry about squirrels carrying it off; they are more interested in finding edible things. It's fun to watch goldfinches picking at

Goldfinch in winter pluumage

the nesting material; they do tend to be more wary around that than the feeder. I think the reason is that they don't want to reveal where the nesting location is to predators. Flying off in a certain direction with a bill full of cotton can be a little conspicuous. If goldfinches catch me watching them eating, they rarely fly off unless I start dancing and flailing my arms. If they are on the nesting material ball and see me they fly off far away.

Female goldfinch

Apartment Birder Tip

Goldfinches will readily eat sunflower hearts. Because they aren't as messy as Nyjer, they're ideal for apartment feeding.

House Finch

Male House Finch

This is a bird that people in the eastern half of the United States are not supposed to be able to see. House Finches were considered a West Coast species up until the 1940s. Then some people started selling them illegally as pet birds in New York under the name of the "Hollywood Finch." As word caught on that the finches were native species and therefore could not be sold as pets, many birds were released in New York. Before long the adaptable House Finches were breeding and by the 1970s had expanded their range as far as North Carolina and Indiana. By the late 1980s they were found in Minnesota and now they are common feeder birds. Though they look similar to Purple Finches, House Finches are now the more common of the two birds at the feeder in urban areas.

Attracting House Finches

House finch chicks will sometimes leave a messy ring of fecal material around the outer cup of their nest.

House Finches are attracted by a variety of foods including sunflower in or out of the shell, safflower and Nyjer. They will also eat specialty foods such as mealworms and orange halves.

House Finches love to nest near our homes and are often the species nesting on holiday wreaths left out too long or in hanging plant baskets. There's little need to worry about disturbing House Finches on the nest as they grow quite accustomed to human activity.

If you find one nesting in your hanging plant baskets, get a small plastic dish like one used for sour cream or chip dip, clean it out thoroughly, punch small holes in the bottom for drainage and then simply lift the nest out of the basket into the plastic dish and place back in the plant basket. The dish will offer protection to the nest when you water the plant.

House Finches are not supposed to use a nest box, but I wouldn't put it past this adaptable species to use one in a pinch. They will use a nesting ledge or a Barn Swallow nest cup. I used to say that House Finches are not cavity nesters, but I once saw a photo of a House Finch nest built inside one of those roosting pouches made of straw that domestic finches will use for nesting. The opening was very wide, perhaps two inches in diameter so it was more of a nesting ledge than a traditional nest pouch, but a step closer to cavity nesting nonetheless.

Female House Finch

White-breasted and Red-breasted Nuthatches

Red-breasted Nuthatch

There are two types of nuthatches that can show up at feeders. The most common is the larger White-breasted Nuthatch. The other is the Red-breasted Nuthatch. One of the folk names for these birds is the rump-up, which refers to their habit of going down a tree headfirst (or rump up). Nuthatches go down trees instead of up as a means for searching for food that woodpeckers miss.

Attracting nuthatches

Nuthatches are fond of sunflower in and out of the shell, safflower, peanuts and suet. You can also attract them with mealworms. Like chickadees, nuthatches will eat out of almost any feeder. Many decorative feeders that birds cling to are ideal for nuthatches. I notice that in most yards I visit, nuthatches seem to prefer the wire mesh feeders.

Nuthatches love suet.

Nuthatches are cavity nesters, but rarely use a nest box. If they do use one, the hole needs to be an inch and a quarter, which is the same size as a House Sparrow, so I wonder if aggressive competition from that non-native species is what keeps them out of nest boxes. I have heard theories that attaching bark to a nest box makes it more attractive to nuthatches, but have not tried it myself.

White-breasted Nuthatches will sometimes carry food away and hide it for later.

CHAPTER NINE

Top Ten Problem Guests

So you're opening up an all-you-can-eat buffet in your yard by providing a bird feeding station. Some guests will wait their turn, eat a little bit and move on, maybe even sing a pleasant song or two. Others will elbow their way in, make obnoxious screeches, destroy property or even eat some of the other guests! You will have some problems at the feeding station. Some will be easy to solve, others will be complex and downright frustrating. You will have to make tough choices or just learn to live with certain birds or critters.

Squirrels

Fox Squirrel

Squirrels will show up at bird feeders. I am always amazed by the number of people who, when they purchase feeders for the first time and are asked about how they intend to handle squirrels, answer, "We don't really have any squirrels in our neighborhood." Just an FYI, if you give this answer in a bird store, the staff will laugh at your naiveté (and expense) after you leave.

You can try to pay off the squirrel mob with a little bribery. Some people find that setting food down in a separate and convenient area can keep squirrels at bay. This method is also very effective if you keep plain safflower and Nyjer in all your bird feeders. Safflower and Nyjer are the squirrels' least favorite foods, so coupling them with some corn on the ground can be a workable situation.

Keep in mind that there are several feeders designed not only to feed squirrels, but to keep you entertained as well. Some of the most popular include the cob of corn attached to a bungee cord or the "squirrel under glass feeder" where the squirrel must crawl into a glass jar to get the food. Just tell a wild bird store employee that you want to feed squirrels and you demand entertainment at the same time; they will help you out.

If you just don't want 'em around, there are several methods to use when it comes to squirrels. The same method doesn't always work in every backyard so you may have to experiment for a bit before you find a system that works. See page 34-37 for guidelines for placing poles and baffles.

Black Squirrel a.k.a. Melanistic Gray Squirrel

Gray Squirrel

Albino Gray Squirrel

If you are attaching your feeders to a deck (squirrels will find a way to your deck; you may not think so, but they will), or if your yard is heavily wooded or is small and fenced, a baffle system may not be an option for you. In these cases you will want to consider a weight-sensitive or other squirrel-resistant feeder. These feeders come in a variety of shapes and sizes and prices. Like anything in life, you get what you pay for. You may find a good deal on a cheap squirrel-proof feeder, but remember how smart the critter is that you are dealing with. A good squirrel-proof feeder will have a squirrel damage war-

Red Squirrel

ranty to back it up. Ask a bird store employee which they would buy; they will give you an honest and experienced answer. After all, they've been there on the front lines with the squirrels.

Examples of squirrel-proof feeders

The Eliminator is weight-sensitive to keep squirrels from accessing the food and allow cardinals to chow down.

» **Weight-Sensitive:** These feeders will close off feeding ports when anything too heavy sits on the perches. Birds have hollow bones for flight and are much lighter than squirrels. Most of these styles of feeders work incredibly well and attract almost all seed-eating songbirds.

» **Cage Style Feeders:** These are tube-style feeders with a wire cage around them to keep squirrels out. These feeders require some patience. It takes a while for birds to get used to going inside the cage to get the food. Most new feeders take a month or less to get birds coming, but I know people who have introduced cage feeders and waited six months to a year to get birds used to the idea of going inside. Another point to consider is that cardinals are too large to fit inside the cage feeders and red squirrels are small enough to sneak in. However, if you're not attracting cardinals anyway, this might be a good bet for you.

Cage-style feeders can take a while for birds to figure out—on rare occasions it can take several months.

» Electrified Feeders: Some feeders on the market are designed so that when a mammal touches two metal pieces on the feeder, they receive a mild shock from a nine-volt battery. They are not lethal, but give enough of an unpleasant jolt to make the animal not want to touch them again. The majority of people who have these feeders love them, but on rare occasions squirrels figure out where to hold onto the feeder without getting shocked.

Squirrel Relocation Programs

Some people try live trapping and either kill or relocate the squirrels. I have yet to see this method work in keeping squirrels out of the yard.

Trapping and removing squirrels rarely results in a squirrel-free yard.

First, when people do this they often share with bird store employees where they are relocating the squirrels. I've got a news flash: you guys are just spreading them around to each other. One customer who lives near Bryant Park will tell us that he drives the squirrels twenty miles west to Carver Park. A customer who lives next to Carver Park tells us that he drives twenty miles east and drops them off at Bryant Park.

Second, when you take one squirrel out of your yard, that leaves a vacancy. Young squirrels being kicked out of a neighboring territory will gladly fill that vacancy. Many people think that removing a squirrel from their yard to a park is the humane thing to do. But a squirrel newly deposited in a park is at great risk for predation in an unfamiliar territory. It must also try to find food in a strange area and fight to the death for an established squirrel's territory.

Getting rid of one chipmunk only leaves a vacancy for a new one.

Third, it just doesn't work. I've known customers who have trapped squirrels until the cows come home and the bushy tailed critters still reside in the yard. One gentleman trapped ninety squirrels in one year, only to discover that for all his effort and mileage he still had squirrels in his yard.

Apartment Birder Tip

Tube-style, weight-sensitive feeders (see opposite page) work great for keeping squirrels from taking over a feeding station mounted on a deck or suspended from a window frame.

Grease

Greasing poles is a popular method of critter control and has been used by bluebird landlords for years to keep raccoons and snakes from climbing nest box poles. A common mistake first-time greasers make is using cooking grease like Crisco or vegetable oil. Do not use edible grease, it just serves as a magnet to squirrels and raccoons. Oftentimes the critters will lick it off and then climb the pole to finish off the bird seed and suet.

A popular grease is black lithium grease that can be spread on with a sponge. Black is the most popular because it's the same color as the poles. I know several people who use it and have to reapply it only two or three times a year. There are some who say that the grease is not safe, but like the red dye or peanut butter issue there is no scientific evidence to support this. I have heard people claim that birds will get the grease on their feathers and not be able to fly. There is no way a bird is going to get grease on its feathers unless you grab the bird and rub it on the pole.

If you are concerned about lithium grease, you can use petroleum jelly (although you will have to reapply it more often) or axle grease. Both of those will also cause critters to slide down a pole.

Raccoons

Raccoons are most active at night.

I get a kick out of people who find knocked-over feeders in the morning, or suet feeders that disappear in the night and when you say, "Sounds like a raccoon," they get an appalled look on their face and exclaim, "We don't have raccoons in our yard." There's no shame in having raccoons in your yard. Lots of nice folks just like you have them. Raccoons are as prolific as squirrels and no matter if your setting is rural or urban you have raccoons in your yard at night. You don't usually see them, but you do see evidence of their visits.

Raccoons will remove bungee cord to get at food stored in garbage cans.

Raccoons are harder to deal with than squirrels. They are bigger and have dexterous hands like human hands and are able to open or carry away almost any type of bird feeder. If you have raccoons making nightly visits to your deck, it's virtually impossible to keep them away. The method that apparently works best is taking in deck feeders at night so raccoons will not have access to them. See page 34-37 for a pole system that has a chance against raccoons.

Blackbirds

Many people refer to the smaller dark birds in their yard as blackbirds. This usually means either Common Grackles, European Starlings or Red-winged Blackbirds. Since these are different birds, different methods are needed to deal with them.

European Starling

Starlings can only eat seed that has been removed from its shell.

European Starlings are non-migratory, but have very different seasonal plumages. In summer, the European Starling is a shiny black bird with green iridescence in its feathers, orange legs and a yellow bill. In winter, they look like a completely different bird with black legs and bill and black feathers with white speckles. They look so different that many people think they have a new bird in their yard and are quite embarrassed when you reveal that they are marveling over a starling.

Starlings were introduced in the late 1800s by the American Acclimatization Society in an effort to bring all of the birds mentioned in the works of William Shakespeare to North America. Less than one hundred starlings were introduced at the time and now we have an overabundance.

Starlings have a tendency to visit yards in large, noisy flocks, discouraging other birds from visiting feeders when they are present. They are also capable of driving native species such as Eastern Bluebirds and Northern Flickers from nest holes in order to use the nest cavity.

Starlings are omnivores and will eat a variety of food from insects and fruit to suet and bird seed. However, there is a weakness. Starlings are unable to crack open any seed with a hard shell, such as black-oil sunflower, striped sunflower, safflower, white millet and peanuts in the shell. Most other songbirds have no trouble eating these seeds, so you can still attract a great variety of species while avoiding the troublesome starling.

Starlings also have a fondness for suet and a large flock of starlings can sometimes drive away woodpeckers, chickadees and nuthatches. Some people find success keeping starlings at bay by feeding plain suet as opposed to nut- and fruit-flavored

Starling in winter plumage

suet. You can purchase suet feeders that require birds to hang on the bottom of the feeder in order to get at the suet. Woodpeckers, chickadees and nuthatches have no problem with this feat, whereas most starlings find this a difficult task.

Some people truly love starlings. Technically, since starlings are an introduced species, they can be kept as pets. But I wouldn't recommend it. Having spent time at a wildlife rehabilitation facility, I can say that they are some of the messiest birds, since they love to bathe and tear things apart. But they are incredible mimics, doing the calls of wild birds and can even be trained to talk. I remember a Twin Cities pet store trying to sell starlings at $75 a bird! If you ever want to take a walk on the wild side, get on an internet search browser like Google and search for starlings as pets and be prepared to have your mind blown by all the people who love and happily live with starlings in their homes.

Apartment Birder Tip

European Starlings will readily eat food out of the shell. If that is the only type of food you are allowed to offer because of association rules, try leaving the feeder empty for a week to encourage them to move on.

Starlings

As a kid growing up in southern Indianapolis, we would get gigantic flocks of starlings in late summer. We didn't have air conditioning so with the windows open, they were so loud we literally couldn't hear the television. In the evenings we would sit outside and marvel at the flocks. Our neighbor Charly, along with my father, did not care for the large flocks of starlings. Periodically, Charly would pop off his BB gun to startle the flock. It didn't work well, although the effect was downright cool! You would hear the pop of the gun, and instantaneous silence and then a loud "whoosh" as all the thousands of starlings would ascend into the sky at once, circle around the neighborhood and then land and start calling all over again. Charly, I'm sure, thought he was accomplishing something helpful, but the only thing that worked was to wait for dark when the birds would sleep.

I remember one evening sitting outside with my mother and father watching the thousands of starlings. Charly popped off his BB gun, and there was the great silence and then whoosh. As the starlings started their circle, my father shouted, "Atta boy, Charly!" and then as if on cue, a starling pooped on my father's shirt. My mother and I couldn't stop laughing for hours after that.

Common Grackle

Grackles eat a fair number of insects, as well as seed.

Grackles are a native species, and if they weren't so aggressive at feeders could be considered by many to be a strikingly beautiful bird. Grackles are black with a purple head and bluish body. The adults' eyes are yellow.

Grackles are migratory and head south in large flocks in winter. In spring they arrive in huge flocks, emptying seed and suet feeders. As it gets warmer they do eat quite a few insects, but will still show up at feeders for seed and teach their young to feed.

Common Grackles do not let squirrels intimidate them.

Grackles are not fond of safflower or Nyjer. Many people will offer plain safflower in the spring and summer in tray-style feeders, finding that they avoid grackles, starlings and squirrels while still bringing in cardinals, chickadees, nuthatches, House Finches and Mourning Doves. Grackles will try to straddle finch feeders to get access at mixes with fine sunflower chips, but if you offer only Nyjer you can usually keep them out of your finch feeders.

Keep in mind that when you first switch to safflower, it may take a while for the other songbirds to get used to the idea since they are used to finding sunflower in your yard. Birds, like people, are generally not fond of change. Some people hope to get by with just adding more safflower to mixes in order to keep grackles away, but the grackles will simply kick out the safflower to gain access to the food they like.

Grackles do not like the taste of safflower.

Male Red-winged Blackbird

Red-winged Blackbird

Some people enjoy the call of the male Red-winged Blackbird, a shiny black bird with red shoulder patches that when flashed reveal a yellow stripe under the red. Females resemble large sparrows with their brown and streaked plumage. Their call is more of a summer reminder than a robin, a lovely "kon korreeeeeee" or as my friend Ari describes, "This is my tree!" Although my husband says that they sound like me: "Where are my keys?"

One of my favorite things is to watch migratory flocks of Red-winged Blackbirds as they reel and lurch and practically turn on a dime. The flock looks like a graceful undulating blob that is almost hypnotic as it flies back and forth. It's magic.

Female Red-winged Blackbird

However, at the feeder the magic is gone! If you live near any kind of natural water source you are going to get Red-winged Blackbirds and there is no easy way to avoid them. Many blackbirds enjoy safflower as much as House Finches do. Sometimes offering them a tray full of filler seeds like white millet or cracked corn can occupy them for a little bit.

Some people have success keeping them at bay with upside down feeders, like the finch feeders that require goldfinches to hang upside down to get the food or suet feeders that only feed from the bottom. Caged feeders can work, but Red-winged Blackbirds will cling to the side of the cage and try to eat the food that is on the bottom.

As insects become more plentiful the blackbirds eat more of those and less of the bird seed, but in summer months when the nests are full of chicks, they will be a constant presence in the yard. As soon as the chicks learn to fly, they will form large flocks and move around.

American Crow

Fake owls rarely keep birds away. If anything, they attract crows.

Crows are big and black, and can be confused with the Common Raven, but ravens have a deep guttural call and snort. Ravens also have a distinctive wedge-shaped tail when they fly whereas crows have a rounded tail.

I have never met anyone who is ambivalent about crows. People either love them to pieces or would love to cut them to pieces. Crows are a member of the Corvid family, the smartest group of birds in the world. They work cooperatively to find food, watch for predators and raise young. When crows are feeding at a feeder, you will almost always find one high on a tree or building keeping watch and ready to warn the others below of potential danger. When crows visit feeders, people either admire their strut and cleverness or shake their fists in anger as the crows eat food that should be going to cardinals.

Crows will eat any seed they can get their bills on. Favorite foods include corn, peanuts, suet and bread. Since they are so smart, many feeders that keep smaller blackbirds out will not keep crows out. The best thing is to find feeders that have openings that are too small for crows to feed out of or are weight-sensitive and can be adjusted to keep heavier birds and squirrels out.

Crows are omnivores and will eat seed, insects, mice, small rabbits, other birds, eggs and carrion.

Crows cannot eat out of finch feeders, and most tube feeders that do not have trays are too difficult for them to feed from. Crows have a tough time trying to hang upside down, so the suet feeders that feed from the bottom will keep most out.

On occasion, crows will switch from being scavengers and turn into hunters. I have watched crows hop in grass and grab small rodents, wearing them out and eventually hacking at the creature and eating it. One day when I was working at my desk at a bird store I heard a nasal shrieking that sounded like a trapped starling outside the back door. Hoping for a glimpse of our resident Cooper's Hawk, I peeked outside only to discover a crow had captured a small cottontail rabbit and was trying to peck it to death and eat it. There are times when an opportunistic crow will notice a sick, injured or weak bird like a sparrow or Mourning Dove and will kill it and eat it. Does that mean you should get rid of crows in your yard? No. Like hawks, they are doing their part to keep the bird population healthy by looking for weak and ill birds, as well as sick mammals.

Crows will also help birds in your yard. They are the first to notice a predator and their loud warning caws alert everyone in the neighborhood that a predator is nearby. Crows themselves are on the food chain. An inspection of a Great Horned Owl nest will reveal lots of black crow feathers. That's why crows go bonkers when they discover an owl during the day.

The crows in my neighborhood are very wary. They will eat on the ground under the feeder, but will not come up to the window ledge. I have seen the crows in the surrounding trees watch the numerous pigeons on my ledge, but they never come over and feed, even though there is plenty of room for them to do so. Perhaps the flock in my neighborhood has learned that humans are trouble.

Apartment Birder Tip

Because crows are such wary creatures, they tend to avoid window feeders—whether the feeders are suction-cupped to the pane or suspended from a hanger. They just don't trust the humans on the other side of the glass.

Blue Jay

Blue Jays will help warn other feeder birds when a predator, such as a hawk, is nearby.

Blue and white, with a sassy crest, Blue Jays are also a member of the Corvid family and, like crows, are a bird people either love or hate. Personally, I enjoy these birds at the feeder. Jays are noisy birds that give their signature "jay jay" call before heading to feeders. Because this is such a loud call, many birds scatter when they hear it. Blue Jays, like crows, will mob hawks and owls or call out when other predators are in the neighborhood. Their calls serve as a warning to other birds to lay low when danger is near.

I think one of the main reasons why Blue Jays are so reviled is that a painting by John James Audubon shows a trio of jays gleefully ingesting songbird eggs, practically giddy in their gluttony as they devour another bird's children, like a bunch of frat boys with a beer keg. Many of us see this image in old bird books and the image sticks in our mind. Every bird has a dark side—and it's not just Blue Jays that eat other birds' eggs—but Blue Jays seem to bear the brunt of the blame.

Blue Jay

Blue Jays are omnivores and eat insects, seed, suet and fruit. Blue Jays are particularly fond of peanuts, corn and sunflower seeds. Being a larger bird with a sharp bill, they are capable of eating peanuts in the shell, which can be quite a show. Blue Jays will fly to a feeder filled with peanuts in the shell, then pick up two or three and let each one drop. Studies have shown that the jays are testing which nut weighs most (and likely contains the most nutmeat). In the end, a Blue Jay will fly away with the heaviest peanut it can find.

Blue Jays gather food, hold it in their crops, and fly away to store it for another day. A full crop can give Blue Jays a "Dolly Parton" appearance.

Blue Jays, like chickadees, will also cache food. Some people are concerned the Blue Jays come in and eat all the food. What they are doing is grabbing several seeds at once and storing them in their crop. They will fly away and store them in places on the ground, in crevices of trees or any other nook or cranny.

Blue Jays are only at a feeder for short periods of time and while they are there, other birds will lay low. Once the Blue Jays move on the other birds will return to the feeder. You will notice this same type of behavior when cardinals are feeding. Blue Jays will offer protection to the birds visiting your feeders when they see a hawk or cat come into the territory by warning the others with their loud calls and diving at the potential predator to get them to move on. You can't keep Blue Jays from visiting your yard, but if you want to distract them from certain feeders try offering whole corn and peanuts in the shell in another part of your yard. If you're concerned that squirrels will eat it all, don't worry; Blue Jays have a way of holding their own against squirrels.

House Sparrow

Male House Sparrow

House Sparrows are another introduced species. They were first brought over in the 1850s for various reasons in different parts of the United States. Some were released as a way to combat insects that were damaging crops and others were released by sentimental settlers who enjoyed seeing the birds that reminded them of their homeland.

Like starlings, House Sparrows are an aggressive and adaptable species. They eat a variety of seeds and will nest in any cavity that has an opening of at least an inch and a quarter in diameter. They have caused many problems with cavity nesters in the United States. House Sparrows have a large, strong, notched bill and will use it to destroy eggs, kill chicks and adult birds by pecking holes in the backs of their heads to take over a nesting cavity.

House Sparrows will be in your yard and there is nothing you can do to keep them out. They are particularly fond of white millet, but will also eat sunflower, cracked corn and peanuts. Some people find that feeding plain safflower keeps House Sparrows at bay, but I have found that my House Sparrows will eat it when desperate.

For some, offering a little bribery to House Sparrows in the form of millet or other cheap feed in a tray feeder in a separate part of the yard is a way to keep them from bothering the rest of the feeders.

You can hang a baffle above your feeders and on the four corners of the baffle attach fishing line. The fishing line should extend a couple of inches below the feeder. On each end of fishing line attach a weight or sinker to keep the line hanging straight. This is not noticeable to you or other birds, but it disturbs House Sparrows. They can tell that something is there, but are unsure of what it is and it interferes with their ability to watch for predators.

A homemade house sparrow deterrent is to hang fishing line from four corners of your feeder or hanging squirrel baffle.

It's tough trying to discourage House Sparrows from nesting. The best thing is to eliminate places for them to nest, like any nest boxes that have an entrance hole wider than an inch and an eighth. Take down vacant multi-compartment birdhouses such as Purple Martin houses. Some places sell House Sparrow houses and you will find them in various neighborhoods. If there is one in your neighborhood, find out who owns it and see if you can have it taken down and replaced by birdhouse more suitable to the native birds in the area. Also, check around your home and see if there are any

Female House Sparrow

gaps in the siding or the eaves of your home that are wide enough for House Sparrows to squeeze into and nest.

There is one final and controversial way to control House Sparrows: trapping and removing them. Like European Starlings and Rock Pigeons, House Sparrows are non-native and unprotected by state and federal laws and it is legal to trap and humanely kill them. Some people are very much against this and feel it is unreasonable and cruel to kill birds that have been here for hundreds of years. I know, I have struggled with it for years. One day I was birding and came across a freshly dead White-breasted Nuthatch. I picked up the carcass to look it over, and on the back of the bird's head was a small hole pierced through the skull into the brain. I looked up from where I found the dead nuthatch and found a small hole. Within minutes a male House Sparrow poked its head out.

House Sparrows are known for this behavior, especially among people who keep bluebird trails. If a House Sparrow wants the nest cavity badly enough it will fight the original owner for the territory. The House Sparrow will wait until a bluebird goes into the box, land on top of the bluebird and then peck the back of the bird's head until it pierces the skull and kills it. House Sparrows will kill the adults, the chicks and smash the eggs; since they are smaller than bluebirds, they have the advantage to move around quicker inside the nest box. After the deed is done, House Sparrows will be in such haste to build the nest that they will sometimes leave the carcasses inside and build the nest on top of them. Because of this, I can understand someone's reasons for trapping and killing House Sparrows. There are a variety of live traps that you can purchase to get House Sparrows, but you must watch them closely to ensure that you get House Sparrows and not other species like Song Sparrows, Fox Sparrows, Black-capped Chickadees or any other native species that might sneak into the cage.

Once you have the sparrows, it will be up to you to find a humane way to euthanize them. You can't drive them five miles away and release them; they will just find their way back to your yard. Never use poison, it could take out the wrong birds.

Canada Geese can quickly become yard nuisances. Feed them at your own risk.

Canada Goose

Canada Geese are a success story that got a little too successful. In the seventies and early eighties you never saw them, especially in large numbers. As the U.S. Fish and Wildlife Service began to reintroduce them, they once again settled in areas where there was water. Now in many cities Canada Geese are overpopulated. In the Twin Cities, lakes sometimes have to be closed off to swimmers because of toxic levels of fecal bacteria deposited by the geese.

Part of the problem is overfeeding. It's true that birds don't rely on bird feeders, but in places such as city parks, several people can come in during the course of a day with loaves of bread, bags of chips and bags of corn. With several people doing it in one day this can give the geese a false impression of the food supply. A lake with enough natural food to support two pairs of Canada Geese raising chicks will sometimes have ten to fifteen pairs raising goslings.

Canada Geese will nest in yards that offer steady food supplies.

A temptation for many people when they see geese returning in the spring is to increase the amount of corn on the ground. It's important not put out too much so you don't encourage them to stay and nest in your neighborhood.

Canada Geese are not fond of kites, so if you are on a large lake with lots of wind, try setting up kites on your docks or the edge of the lake. There are some models designed to look like life-size Bald Eagles and Ospreys, and these are especially effective at keeping Canada Geese out of yards where they are not wanted.

The bottom line is to not feed them. Talk to neighbors and try to work out a plan together. It's worthwhile to keep their numbers down. Some states have a roundup program that will send teams of people to neighborhoods with problem geese. Adult Canada Geese are flightless for a period in summer as they shed old feathers and grow in new ones. This usually coincides with when they have young. As the young are just growing in their flight feathers, the teams will round them up with nets and cart them away. From there they are slaughtered for use in homeless shelters and food shelves. In some ways this can be viewed as urban farming. If you're not comfortable with that, don't feed geese.

Cats

Cats kill prey for fun, taking food away from natural predators.

Overall, songbird populations are declining every year. People are always looking for a cause and fast and easy fix. The bottom line is that there is no one cause (unless you want to count the human race, but we're not going to get rid of ourselves). Some people blame cell phone towers, some blame migratory and nesting habitat destructions, some blame urban sprawl, forest and prairie fragmentation, pesticides, crows, hawks, cats. The truth is, it's all of these. Are we going to fix all of these problems overnight? Of course not; it's going to take baby steps. Outdoor cats are certainly one of the major factors for songbird declines, but they are not the only cause. Cats are a touchy issue and dealing with cats stalking birds at a feeding station needs to be handled with lots of tact and patience.

I know many people who feed birds and let their cats roam outdoors. There are a small minority of cats that do not chase and kill birds, but most do, and even if it's one bird here and there, that really adds up. I find that most people who feed birds and let their cats run around outside to kill birds are just turning a blind eye to it.

Cat television!

If the guilty feline is not yours, but you know whose it is, you'll have to take a different tack. Talk to your neighbor first. Let them know that you have a yard with feeders and that the cat is sitting under the feeders either killing the birds or scaring them away. Ask if the neighbor could think of a compromise. Realize that the chances of your neighbor saying, "Oh, I will never let my cat out of the house again" are incredibly slim. If a cat has known a life outdoors and is suddenly forced to only be indoors, it's incredibly difficult to keep that cat happy. So, be prepared for some compromise. See if the neighbor will let the cat out only at night when birds will not be at the feeder. Or ask your neighbor if the cat could be out from noon until four when bird activity is low.

If the neighbor is not agreeable to that, find out what the pet ordinance is for your city or county. Many cities have laws that require pets to be restrained by the owner when outdoors or that pets may not leave the owner's property. In that case, a few calls to animal control is usually enough to keep the cat from coming into your yard again.

Some people resort to threatening neighbors or harming cats to keep them out of the yard. This actually does more harm than good. I know one person who would set out a live trap for neighbors' cats. The first time the cat went in the trap, the person would walk to the cat owner's home with the cat and explain that the cat was trapped under some bird feeders. This time the cat was being returned to the owner. The next time the cat would disappear. That doesn't help the neighborhood.

If the neighbor is not willing to control the cat in any way, try setting up some barriers near your feeders. Chain-link fencing around ground feeding areas, brush piles and birdbaths can be effective keeping cats out, while allowing birds to fly freely in and out of the space. Keep in mind that cats are capable of jumping quite high, so fencing over the top may be necessary to keep them from jumping into the enclosure.

Keep feeding stations twenty feet or more away from brush piles or bushes so birds have time to fly away when a cat starts an attack.

Another effective technique can be setting your sprinkler to face bushes where cats hide to stalk their prey. Cats don't like to hide in wet, drippy areas.

If the cats are wild or feral cats being dumped in the neighborhood, try to find out if there are any organizations in your area that rehabilitate feral cats. Some organizations will euthanize cats that are not suitable for indoor pets, some will neuter and then release them back to the wild (which really doesn't solve the problem) and others will do their darndest to find the cats indoor homes. While there are groups that will come and live trap cats, they tend to fill to capacity quickly and often refuse to take any new cats. If you find an organization that will handle feral cats, you can try live trapping the wild felines.

The bottom line is that cats in the yard are not an easy situation to deal with and will require some effort and creativity on your part to keep them from eating birds at your feeder.

Apartment Birder Tip

Keeping cats indoors makes the world safer for songbirds. But that doesn't mean your cat can't enjoy the birds as much as you do. Cats are greatly entertained by watching birds at window feeders; in fact, "bird watching" is a great way to keep *Kitty* happy while you're away from home.

Hawks

Immature Cooper's Hawk

When you set up a bird feeding station you will attract birds. That's the whole idea, of course. But along with the songbirds you've invited, your feathered visitors will invariably include predatory birds as well. Some will be after the mice, chipmunks and squirrels that come to the feeder, but most are going to be after the birds that come to your feeder.

When this happens, some people get concerned that they are setting a trap for songbirds and want to quit feeding them. The fact is that predatory birds would be hunting the birds whether you are feeding them or not. Hawks look for large flocks of birds congregating in feeding areas such as orchards, fields and berry trees. Songbirds were hunted before you ever put up a feeder and will continue to be hunted long after you take your feeder down. What's different is that when a feeding station is put up you have set up a situation where you are able to watch the hunting.

The most common hawks to show up to feeding stations are members of the Accipiter family, such as the Sharp-shinned Hawk and the larger Cooper's Hawk. These are slender hawks that have long tails and short wings. They are designed to fly short distances at great speed and are experts at maneuvering among dense wooded areas and thickets. Accipiters were made to hunt fast-flying songbirds. I think of accipiters as birds that act first and think second, as they have a tendency to fly into windows when hunting small songbirds.

Adult Sharp-shinned Hawk

If you are concerned about hawks, you can try to provide cover at least ten feet from your feeding station. You don't want it any closer than that or squirrels will use it as a springboard to your feeders, or if there is a cat in the neighborhood, it might use the cover as a hideout for hunting your birds.

Apart from that there's not much else to be done. Take heart, the hawk will not completely rid your yard of birds. While the hawk is perched, birds will hide, but once it moves on, birds will resume feeding. Hawks only take what they need to survive and will never completely deplete the food supply. Hawks have a tendency to hunt the weak and injured, since that is the prey that is easiest to catch, and this helps prevent the spread of disease to other birds.

Shrikes, the non-raptors

Unlike raptors, shrikes do not kill their prey with talons, but with their bill.

Have you ever been walking by a barbed wire fence and noticed some grasshoppers or half-eaten rodents sticking to the barbs? Maybe on a thorny bush you found a half-eaten finch jammed onto some thorns. Are these the works of some weirdo in the neighborhood? Probably not! It is likely the work of a shrike.

There are two types of shrikes in North America: the Loggerhead Shrike and the Northern Shrike. They resemble each other. To me, they resemble chickadees on steroids. Though these are predatory birds, they are not the same as hawks, owls, falcons and eagles, which are raptors. The word raptor comes from the Latin *raptus*, which means one who seizes. Raptors such as eagles, hawks, owls and falcons use their powerful toes to grab or seize their food. Shrikes do not have strong toes and have to land on their prey and subdue it, usually by biting it several times. From there, the shrike will fly to its territory, impale the prey and hack at the carcass when it is hungry. Because of this habit, the shrike is sometimes known as the butcherbird.

Shrikes aren't common, but occasionally they will show up at the feeder looking to feed on small rodents or small birds. Some people have even found shrikes feeding on the suet of their suet feeders. It's usually not a bird that sticks around, so consider yourself lucky if you spot one, it's a cool bird to see.

Rock Pigeon

Rock Pigeon

In many ways, pigeons are harder to deal with than squirrels. Rock Pigeons (as they are officially called) are incredibly smart and break many bird feeding rules. Usually large birds like this have a tough time feeding on clinging style feeders, but I have watched them straddle feeders and use their wings to maintain balance on even the tiniest of feeders. They learn by watching each other, so once one pigeon figures out a feeder, the rest of the flock will soon follow suit.

Pigeons can be a nuisance as they have large crops and will eat a huge amount of any food including suet. Also, if they roost on your house, the buildup of excrement can be a health hazard. It's best to try to nip a pigeon problem in the bud. The longer you let them go, the larger the flock gets and the harder it is to deter them.

If pigeons are roosting on your house, you want to block the area where they are roosting. If this is under an overhang, you can put up screening similar to the kind used to keep birds off berry producing plants. You can also try a sticky substance called Tanglefoot that is uncomfortable for them to stand on. There are also metal and plastic spikes that can be put on rafters that are uncomfortable for pigeons to sit on.

If they are visiting your feeders, eliminate ground feeding and all tray feeding. If that doesn't work, look into getting a really good squirrel-resistant feeder. A good feeder is one with an adjustable counterbalance. Feeders I have seen that keep pigeons out are Brome's Squirrel Buster II, the Droll Yankee Tipper, the Absolute Squirrel Proof Feeder, the Jonboy Deluxe Feeder and the Colibri Squirrel Be Gone. I have seen all other seed feeders conquered by pigeons.

Apartment Birder Tip

The same weight-sensitive hanging feeders that do such a good job keeping squirrels at bay also work well preventing pigeons from taking over an urban feeding station.

CHAPTER TEN

Surprise Guests

My friend, Neil, is British and has a fabulous yard I love to experiment with. One spring I looked out his window and noticed a very blue chickadee on his peanut feeder. The little hamster in my head started turning its wheel: that was no chickadee, that was a Blue Tit. Through a remarkable coincidence, I had a camera and captured some footage of the bird. I showed it to Neil who didn't seem surprised and told me how he'd always seen them as a kid back home. I tried to explain how unlikely it was to have a Blue Tit in the Upper Midwest, but he never really got it. I guess it just goes to show that a good bird can show up anytime, anywhere.

Sometimes you will be completely surprised by what shows up at your feeders, especially during migration. Always be on the lookout for something cool that could be visiting you at any time.

OPPOSITE: Black Bear

Flying Squirrels

Northern Flying Squirrel

These nocturnal creatures are said to be as common as gray squirrels, but since they only come out at night, we rarely notice them. Flying squirrels are most likely to visit in the winter, but I have had them visit a feeder year-round. They are surprisingly tolerant of humans and some people have gotten these critters to feed from their hands. Because of their small size and ability to glide long distances, it's impossible to keep them out of bird feeders, but with their small size they don't eat nearly the same amount as squirrels, raccoons or even chipmunks.

Most people enjoy feeding flying squirrels and favorite foods include peanuts, mixed nuts, sunflower seeds, peanut butter suet and mealworms. From time to time, flying squirrels will use bird houses for nesting or raising young.

Indigo Bunting

A Painted Bunting shares this feeder with three Indigo Buntings, including a plain, brown female. Buntings are among the few species that love to eat white millet.

Indigo Buntings are the type of bird that will get almost anyone interested in birds. Small and sneaky in shrubs, they can be easily overlooked, but once someone sees them at the feeding station they become obsessed with keeping this dark blue bird in the neighborhood. Male Indigo Buntings are technically black, but their feathers reflect blue light and appear deep indigo blue at the feeder. Female Indigo Buntings are one of the most drab birds on the planet. They are brown with no streaking, spotting or anything. Sometimes there can be a hint of blue on their wings but they are generally brown, brown, brown.

Indigo Buntings are like grosbeaks, typically showing up at feeders during migration when the insects aren't out in full force yet. They can come up to finch feeders filled with Nyjer or sunflower chips. Nothing is quite as beautiful as looking at a finch feeder in spring with the perches full of bright yellow male goldfinches and accented by a couple of male Indigo Buntings.

Indigo Buntings are most commonly found on the ground underneath the feeders eating white millet. Spring and fall are the best times to offer millet if for no other reason than to attract these

Male Indigo Buntings look dark blue in the sun and almost black in the shade.

colorful insectivores. Buntings usually nest at the edge of an open field near water. If one takes residence in your yard you will probably see them all summer, but most only see them during migration.

Not only are Indigo Buntings beautiful, males are the most dedicated singers and are often the only bird singing in the dog days of summer in the middle of the afternoon.

Scarlet Tanager

Scarlet Tanager

"Good grief! How red do you have to be?" That is one of my favorite descriptions a customer gave me of a male scarlet tanager. This species is one of the most vividly colorful birds you will ever see in your life. Males are a brilliant scarlet red with black wings. Females are yellow with black wings. Scarlet Tanagers nest high in the tops of oak trees and are more often heard than seen. The song resembles that of a robin, only buzzier, and they will also give characteristic chip note that sounds like the birds are saying "chick burr."

Tanagers are primarily insectivores, but when they return to breeding grounds in the spring, and there's a strong cold snap, they will check out bird feeding stations in search of protein. When desperate, tanagers will feed on sunflower chips, peanut butter, fruit and nut-flavored suets, dried fruit such as raisins, oranges, grape jelly and, of course, mealworms. As soon as the weather warms up and insects are out in full force, tanagers will return to the tops of trees, rarely to be seen for the rest of the summer.

Wild Turkey

Wild Turkey

Wild Turkey populations have really grown quite large in the last several years. As more and more turkeys show up in the wild, the more tolerant of humans they are becoming. Turkeys will wander around several neighborhoods in flocks in search of food. They'll eat most any kind of seed but especially enjoy whole and cracked corn, nuts, dried fruit, pumpkin seeds, mealworms and sunflower seeds. I wonder if they will become the next Canada Goose.

As turkeys grow comfortable in a neighborhood, they will sometimes walk right up to windows and peer inside homes to see what's going on. They will even fly onto decks if there is a readily available food source. As turkeys are wild birds, it's important to give them their space, especially during the breeding season. When it feels threatened, a cornered turkey might launch an attack.

Turkeys are becoming very urban.

Ring-necked Pheasant

Pheasants pop up from time to time in neighborhoods in search of corn and other seeds. Pheasants tend to be more skittish than other birds, as they are tasty creatures and humans love to hunt them. They will often show up in newly constructed open areas skulking about under bird feeders and keeping a hairy eyeball open for intruding humans.

Male pheasants are striking birds with green heads with a red wattle and a tail about as long as their bodies. They tend to enjoy the same foods as Wild Turkeys including whole and cracked corn, nuts, dried fruit, pumpkin seeds and sunflower seeds. They like to hide in cover before approaching the bird feeder.

White-tailed Deer

Like frat boys at a beer keg, deer love bird feeders.

As urban areas spread out, deer are becoming a more common sight in backyards, even on busy streets. Deer eat everything. Just in case you didn't catch that the first time, let me rephrase it: Deer eat everything! They love bird seed of any flavor and will tip a tube feeder and chug the seed like a frat boy with a beer bong. Some people have such a problem with deer eating from their feeders that they must hang the feeders high in the air. Deer will even stand on their hind legs to get at a good sunflower mix, so if you have severe deer trouble, make sure feeders are at least ten feet off the ground.

Some people enjoy feeding deer extra corn or wildlife mixes in the winter, but they might be opening a can of worms. Most people who feed birds enjoy gardening. Many of us have neighbors who garden until the cows come home. Deer love to munch on gardens and no amount of supplemental feeding will keep them from having a fresh salad.

Deer in metro areas have no natural predators and are often at the mercy of vehicles. Car-deer collisions can be fatal not only for the deer, but for the humans involved as well. In the long run, it's best not to encourage deer, no matter how cute they look.

Warblers

Warblers are the colorful little birds that many a birdwatcher lives for in the spring. There are several species of warblers and all are primarily

Common yellow throat

Yellow Warbler

Yellow-rumped Warbler

insectivores that don't typically visit feeders. They are attracted by other birds' activity, so, during migration, warblers may unexpectedly visit feeding stations. If the weather is cold, they may stick around and try to eat suet and dried fruit or visit birdbaths. If we are having a severe cold snap, you can easily supplement warbler diets with live mealworms.

Native Sparrows

Some people will look out at the little brown jobs under the feeder and think "Ugh, all I get is House Sparrows." Others will look closely at the mass of brown and periodically notice that some of those brown guys are a different type of brown than the others. This isn't just geekery; there are exciting sparrows to be seen at the bird feeder. Seriously, there are!

Song Sparrow

North America is host to several species of sparrows that don't crowd out other birds and can be a fun addition under any feeder. Native sparrows will scratch the ground looking for white millet, Nyjer, cracked corn and sunflower chips. Some sparrows will only be here in winter, some will only be under feeders during migration and others will only be summertime visitors.

Pet Birds

You may find a bird at the feeder that really doesn't belong there. Most of the time, they are escaped exotic birds. These birds can show up at feeders for a variety of reasons, but usually they have either gotten out of the

American Tree Sparrow

home by accident or someone has released their brightly colored bird thinking it desired freedom in the wild as opposed to the security of the cage it had always known as home.

The most common pet birds to show up at feeders include parakeets, cockatiels, finches and lovebirds, but goodness knows there are a host of other species. If you find a pet bird in your yard, do everything you can to capture it. Most pet birds can withstand freezing temperatures for short periods of time, but it's incredibly difficult for a parakeet to survive a true, long winter.

The easiest way to catch a pet bird is to set a cage outside with the door open. Place fresh food and water inside the cage. Most of the time pet birds will go right inside the cage as they recognize it as a source of safety and food. From there, try to find the owners on the chance that the bird got away accidentally. If you cannot find them, you can either keep the bird or take it to your local humane society.

Bears

Bears can be hard on feeders.

Yes, bears—and boy will you be surprised when they show up! Bears treat feeding stations the way the cast of *Animal House* treated a toga party. There is no feeder that will keep bears out. There are a few that claim to have a lifetime warranty against bear damage, but they are made out of cast iron and are incredibly heavy. Bears could still feed out of the ones that I have seen, but would have a tough time ripping them apart.

People who have cabins in remote areas most often have a bear problem, but bears will travel, especially young ones, and more and more we are hearing stories of young bears popping up in metro areas. If you have a bear coming to your feeders, I recommend taking your feeders down or at the very least taking them in at night until the bear moves on. Leaving the feeders out will just encourage the bear to keep visiting.

Do not put extra food out for bears; there's not enough to satiate them and honestly, a fed bear is a dead bear. Feeding bears acclimates them to humans and the more acclimated they become the more at risk they are of being shot for being a nuisance animal.

CHAPTER ELEVEN

Common Questions

Over the years, I've been asked lots of questions about bird feeding and general yard bird care. Some questions crop up more than others, and here they are.

Why aren't there any birds at my feeder?

Depending on the time of year and weather, you will have times of low bird activity. Seasonal movement is a big factor, especially in the spring and fall as some birds may migrate out of an area, and it may be another week or two until other birds migrate in.

Common Redpolls and Pine Siskins.

Another cause of low bird activity can be any kind of construction going on in your yard, especially during nesting season. If you are getting your roof replaced, birds don't want to raise their chicks with that kind of ruckus going on. Also, major landscape changes can upset bird activity. For example, if a large cedar tree that birds used for cover before flying in to your feeder is taken out of the yard, that could cause birds to shift their feeding patterns.

Some people worry that hawks will cause songbirds to abandon a feeding station. It's true that when a raptor such as a Cooper's Hawk or Sharp-shinned Hawk is perched around a feeding station, birds will hide. But soon after the hawk leaves, birds will resume normal feeding activity.

Cats can be a different problem. Once a hawk has hunted a particular spot for a day it will move on to another. Cats that stalk feeding stations for play will sometimes spend hours beneath a feeder. This will cause a decrease in bird activity. Hawks only take what they need for food and then move on. Cats will take a larger volume of prey.

How important is it for me to clean out my bird feeders?

Incredibly important! There are different theories as to how often you should clean out your bird feeders. Some people never do it, some people do it once a season, others once a month and a few once or twice a week. At the very least you need to clean the feeder out once a season and any time you notice a foul smell, mold or clumping.

It's a good idea to clean feeders out after it has been raining. Moisture can get trapped inside of bird feeders and that can lead to disease outbreaks such as salmonella. A good rule of thumb is that if the feeder looks gross to you, birds shouldn't be eating out of it.

Female House Finch

Another overlooked area is under the feeder. Bacteria and mold can spread like wildfire, especially during the wet spring. Rake up empty shells and uneaten seed as often as you can. Keeping bird feeding areas clean is far more important than keeping bird feeders filled on a regular basis. Moldy seed will do far more damage to bird populations than an empty bird feeder.

How do I keep woodpeckers from pecking on my house?

The best tactic is don't buy a house with cedar siding or stucco. Woodpeckers are difficult to keep away, but there are several options to try. What works for one person may not work for the next, so you may have to try a few different methods to find out which one works best for you. It's helpful to know that woodpeckers will peck on houses for one of three reasons.

A little bribery goes a long way with a Downy Woodpecker.

One reason is as a food source. Leaf cutter bees will lay eggs in gaps in cedar siding. When the larvae hatch, woodpeckers can hear them moving and peck to make holes to get at the food source.

The second reason is for nesting. Sometimes siding or stucco can appeal to woodpeckers as an ideal nesting hole. Woodpeckers don't have nearly as much on their minds as humans and get a remarkable amount of work done in a relatively short time. Sometimes, after pecking the hole, woodpeckers discover that the inside isn't as ideal for raising young as they had hoped and will move on. Other birds such as starlings, House Sparrows and chickadees will move into the prospective area quicker than you can say, "Cute fixer-upper."

The third reason is to use a part of your home, such as aluminum gutters or an aluminum chimney, as a drumming post. In the spring, especially at dawn, a male woodpecker finds a nice log to peck (drum) and announces his territory. The louder the drumming, the farther it travels and the better the chance that the male woodpecker will deliver his message. He's basically saying, "Yo, ladies, I'm available, come check out my territory, and other males, stay the heck away." Pecking on aluminum resonates loudly and works great for male woodpeckers, but is less than ideal for most homeowners—especially at dawn.

Whenever you are having a woodpecker problem with your home, it's important to nip it in the bud. The longer you let it go, the harder it is to discourage the birds.

First and most important, patch any holes. Holes on the side of your home are a giant billboard that reads, "some woodpecker found food here once" and "this is a hot nest spot for House Sparrows." Squirt linseed oil inside the hole to try to kill off any insect larvae that might be left inside. Fill the hole with steel wool and then caulk it. You might also have an exterminator check for insects and paint the area with insecticidal paint to help kill insects.

Hang up shiny, moving objects. Woodpeckers don't trust shiny objects and will tend to shy away from them. Hanging holographic windsocks works well and wild bird specialty stores should have a selection. There are also items called Bird Scare Balloons, which are giant beach balls with eyes on them that you can hang outside the affected area. A few people have had success with large wind chimes and other people go for homemade woodpecker repellents in the form of hanging pie tins or empty cans.

There are some motion sensitive devices that drop fake spiders down or squirt water when motion is detected and are very effective at keeping woodpeckers away.

When woodpeckers are using a house as a food source some people have found that providing food such as suet or peanuts in other parts of the yard, as well as patching up the holes, is a way to keep woodpeckers off the house.

It's important to understand that woodpeckers are protected under the Migratory Bird Treaty Act so harming or killing any woodpecker is illegal.

I found a baby bird. What should I do?

This fully feathered goldfinch is less than 48 hours from flying. A bird found with this many feathers should either be put back in the nest or, if it won't stay there, left nearby so the parents can teach it to survive.

Most of the time the very best thing to do is to leave the bird on the ground. Most people find young birds when they are just leaving the nest and learning to fly.

The young birds usually resemble adults with a few spots of down, and they can barely flutter more than a foot or two. This is the bird equivalent of a pimply fifteen-year-old with a learner's permit.

Left alone, these birds are usually flying well within 24 to 48 hours. So if you find a young bird that is on the ground, is fully feathered and is not in immediate danger from a predator like a cat, leave it be. The parents are nearby waiting for you to leave so they can call the bird to the safety of a hiding spot and teach it to forage for itself. Once a baby bird is strong enough to get out of a nest, it is ready to learn to search for food on its own.

If the bird is naked or has mostly pin feathers or quills sticking out, try to locate the original nest. If you can't find it or have found pieces of it on the ground, try to rebuild a nest. Get a plastic dish like a Cool Whip container or cream cheese container. Poke small holes into the bottom of it to allow drainage. If remnants of the original nest are on the ground try to reconstruct the nest inside the plastic dish or try to create a new nest with dry grasses, cotton fibers or pieces of

Albino chickdee fledgling

yarn that are no longer than six inches. Once you have completed the nest, place the baby bird(s) inside the structure and place the new nest as high in the original tree as possible. You may have to secure the nest cup to the tree with screws, nails or cable ties.

Do not worry about the parents abandoning the young if you touch them. Most birds have a lousy sense of smell, and even if they see you holding the chicks, they will not abandon them, but simply wait for you to leave before tending to the young.

If you have found the adult birds dead or if you have watched the young birds hiding for over two hours, then it is time to call a professional, licensed wildlife rehabilitator. You can find them by looking in the phone book under wildlife, calling your local wild bird specialty stores, contacting the humane society, the local U.S. Fish and Wildlife Service office or the local Department of Natural Resources. You can also look up wildlife rehabilitators online by visiting www.wildliferehabilitators.com.

Do NOT raise baby birds on your own. It's incredibly difficult and in the case of most species is illegal without state and federal permits from U.S. Fish and Wildlife. Most baby birds require being fed every half hour, twelve hours day. Also, when birds are young, they imprint on whatever they see feeding them. So if a Blue Jay that was raised by a human sees a human when it reaches sexual maturity, it will try to mate with a human instead of other Blue Jays because that is what it identifies with. Also, humans are ill equipped to teach young birds how to look for tasty insects and how to avoid predators. Many people raise ducklings from game farms and release them in area parks and lakes. Most of these birds have never seen a raccoon or fox and have no idea to avoid them so as not to get eaten.

Diet is also a huge issue. Many believe that bread dipped in milk is a good food source, but in fact it's one of the worst things to feed baby birds. Most, like robins, eat very few seeds and require a huge variety of insects and berries to get proper nutrition. If the young bird manages to survive to adulthood without that specialized diet, it is likely to have severe bone damage and other issues related to malnutrition.

When is it time to put out the feeder and when do I take it in?

Juncos are also called Snowbirds.

The only time to take in your feeder is when you are tired of watching the birds. Wild birds never need bird feeders to survive. Studies show that even in the worst of weather, such as a blizzard, healthy birds use a bird feeder for only 20 percent of their overall diet. They treat bird feeders the way we should treat fast food.

Birds will know to migrate and find other food sources in spring even if you leave your feeder out.

Feeding birds in warmer months can be very rewarding as you watch adult birds bring in the young to teach them how to use your feeding station. Many male songbirds are in their breeding plumage and are incredibly beautiful, natural yard art.

Why aren't the birds using the new birdbath I just purchased?

As a rule, birds do not trust new things. Different is usually bad for birds, so when a new item is introduced at a feeding station, they will naturally be wary. Birds tend to find water by sound like that of the babbling of a brook or trickling of a small waterfall. If you set out your birdbath you need to find ways of making a splashing sound to get their attention. You can purchase recirculation pumps and drippers that plug into an outdoor outlet and create a relaxing sound in your bath. If you have a sprinkler, aim it so that some of the water falls into the bath; that will get the birds' attention.

Sometimes, birds have a tougher time seeing water in lighter colored baths. If you have a light colored birdbath, try placing some darker decorative rocks on the bottom to see if that makes a difference. Birds might also avoid a bath that is too deep for them. An inch and a half of water is sufficient for most birds, so if your bath is deeper, place some rocks in there to add some different levels and make it easier for smaller birds to perch and bathe.

A darker bath is easier for birds to see.

How do I keep birds from hitting my window?

This is not an easy question to answer. Birds strike window panes for different reasons. During mating season, a male will sometimes see his reflection as a rival for his territory and will try to fight the intruder to get it to leave. Migrating birds will see a reflection of the space behind them as they fly and perceive that they will be able to fly ahead only to fatally encounter the hard surface of a window pane. Feeder placement can also play a role in window strikes. In some instances, hawks will drive birds into a window to stun them and make them easier to catch.

There are several options to try, but they're not simple. For birds fighting their own reflection, you need to get them out of the habit of seeing the reflection. Every day, when the bird is inspecting his nesting territory, he comes to the same spot and finds a rival waiting for him. You can get him to forget about this rival by placing a barrier on the outside of the window. Cover the glass with

This male cardinal doesn't realize that its rival happens to be its own reflection.

a bed sheet or newspaper for ten to fourteen days. This might seem like an inconvenience, but it's much better than listening to a bird slamming itself against your window for half the summer.

If birds are flying into the window, look at the location of your bird feeders. Having feeders within ten feet of a window prevents birds from hitting the pane so hard. Having feeders right on your window is even better. A feeder right on the window forces the birds to slow down and inspect a possible feeding area.

Feeders within twelve to thirty feet of the house can cause more bird fatalities. The feeders are far enough away that the birds can get a good speed going before they hit the window. If feeders are more than thirty feet away, that tends to force the birds into a flight path away from the window panes.

If hawks are driving birds into the window, there is not a lot you can do. Birds are trying to flee a predator and if panic sets in, they are not going to make the best flying choices. If this is a regular problem try placing decals, sun catchers, or Mylar tape on the outside of the window to break up the reflection. These need to be on the outside; if they are on the inside, a reflection on the window will block their view.

Another option is getting the type of netting that is used by gardeners to keep birds from eating berry bushes and placing that six inches away from the window pane on the outside. This creates a type of cushion, preventing songbirds from hitting the window. The netting is so fine that it is barely noticeable when you look outside.

My suet feeder completely disappeared overnight. What happened?

If a bird feeder disappears in the night, is dumped on the ground at night or gets obliterated in the night, chances are you have raccoons visiting. It doesn't matter where your yard is; even in the heart of the city you can get raccoons. They are surprisingly more resourceful than squirrels.

One solution is to take your feeders—especially suet or nectar feeders—inside at night. Another option is to quit feeding for two to three weeks to encourage the raccoons to find a different route for food at night.

Raccoons have been known to take suet feeders back to their dens.

In the best situation, mount feeders so that the bottoms of the feeders hang no lower than five feet. Then place a metal canister or baffle that is about two feet long on the pole just under the bird feeders. If the pole is a good eight to ten feet from fences, chairs, trees or bushes this should keep the raccoons off of your bird feeding station. Another option for pole-mounted feeders is to spread black lithium grease on the pole to keep raccoons from climbing it. You want to use lithium and not cooking grease. Cooking grease will only encourage the raccoons to lick it off the pole. See page 34 for a raccoon-proof pole system for decks, and page 132 for more info about this masked bandit.

Is there any seed that squirrels won't eat?

If it's food, squirrels will eat it.

Ha ha ha ha ha, that question kills me every time! Birds love sunflower, peanuts and corn. Alas, so do squirrels. Some people have found success feeding plain safflower, but if a squirrel is hungry enough it will develop a taste for it.

There are pepper-treated seeds, but for every person who says that it works, someone else says that their squirrels love spicy food. The secret to getting it to work is to lightly spray the seed with a cooking oil to get the powdered pepper to stick to the seed better. You might have to clean the feeder more often, since high humidity or excess rain combined with the oil will increase the possibility of mold in the feeder.

Most people find that squirrels generally do not like plain Nyjer. If you mix that with fine sunflower seeds, then the squirrels will eat it, but Nyjer by itself often does not interest a squirrel.

Your best bet for keeping squirrels away is to use a weight-sensitive squirrel-proof feeder. See Chapter Three for squirrel-proof pole mounting options, and page 128-130 for more about squirrel-proof feeders.

I'd like to raise baby ducks or baby pheasants as a project with my kids to help the environment. How do I get started?

Don't get started! Places that sell ducks and pheasants for people to raise and release are generally more interested in making money off the birds than helping the environment.

Remember that baby birds imprint on whatever they see feeding them. So young ducks raised by people will think of themselves more as humans than ducks, and come mating season they are going to be sorely disappointed.

We make lousy parents for birds. We don't teach ducks or pheasants how to hide from predators or what potential predators are. Baby birds don't hatch with that pre-programmed into them, they learn it from the birds raising them. Most pheasants and ducks raised by humans and released in the wild are eaten less than a week after they are released.

A Wood Duck chick leaves the nest.

CHAPTER TWELVE

Case Studies

In this section, I'll take a look at some sample pieces of property and discuss what kinds of birds they can attract and how. This might give you some ideas for your own space.

Case #1

Home with sizeable backyard

A large, wild backyard

» **Habitat nearby:** lots of trees with a water source like a lake or marsh nearby

» **Possible birds:** Northern Cardinal, Black-capped Chickadee, Carolina Chickadee, Mourning Dove, Wood Duck, House Finch, American Goldfinch, Dark-eyed Junco, Mallard, Red-breasted Nuthatch, White-breasted Nuthatch, Baltimore Oriole, Ring-necked Pheasant, American Robin, Barn Swallow, Downy Woodpecker, Hairy Woodpecker, Northern Flicker, Red-bellied Woodpecker, Pileated Woodpecker, Eastern Bluebird, Indigo Bunting, Rose-breasted Grosbeak, Ruby-throated Hummingbird, House Wren, Carolina Wren, White-throated Sparrow, Song Sparrow, Wild Turkey, Red-winged Blackbird, American Crow, Canada Goose, Common Grackle, Brown-headed Cowbird, Blue Jay, House Sparrow, European Starling, Cooper's Hawk, Sharp-shinned Hawk

» **Best bets for feeder types:** finch tube feeder, weight-sensitive sunflower or all-purpose feeders, well protected or baffled suet feeders, upside down finch feeder and suet feeder, mealworm feeder, hummingbird feeder, oriole feeder, cage style feeder

» **Best bets for foods to offer:** Nyjer, sunflower mixes, safflower, suet, peanuts, mealworms, nectar, grape jelly, fruit, cracked and whole corn

» **Best bets for nesting birds:** wren house, chickadee house, Wood Duck house

» **Possible hurdles:** squirrels, raccoons, deer, Red-winged Blackbirds

This type of yard has several bird possibilities and the owner can get a great variety of birds. What needs to be considered is how close the trees are to each other. If they are fairly close together, using a pole system with a baffle may not work since squirrels could jump ten feet from a tree branch over to the feeders. If that is the case, weight-sensitive or caged feeders will need to be considered to keep the critters out. Also, this type of habitat will bring in lots of grackles and blackbirds, so a tray feeder filled with plain safflower might help other birds have a place to eat that the blackbirds won't care for as much.

Deer will be abundant in this yard, so try to mount feeders high up so they cannot eat out of the bird feeders. Some people like to offer corn on the ground for turkeys, ducks, geese and pheasant as well as the deer. Keep that in mind when you're gardening because if the deer are visiting the bird feeders, they will visit the garden too.

Case #2

Apartment building in town

» *Habitat nearby:* few trees and open areas

An urban landscape

» *Possible birds:* Northern Cardinal, Black-capped Chickadee, Carolina Chickadee, Mourning Dove, House Finch, Dark-eyed Junco, Red-breasted Nuthatch, White-breasted Nuthatch, Baltimore Oriole, American Robin, Rock Pigeon, Downy Woodpecker, Hairy Woodpecker, Rose-breasted Grosbeak, Ruby-throated Hummingbird, White-throated Sparrow, Song Sparrow, American Crow, Common Grackle, Blue Jay, House Sparrow, European Starling, Cooper's Hawk, American Kestrel.

» *Best bets for feeder types:* finch feeders, tube style sunflower feeders, weight-sensitive feeders, small suet feeder, hummingbird feeder, mealworm feeder, window feeders

» *Best bets for foods to offer:* Nyjer, sunflower hearts, peanuts, non-melting suet, mealworms, safflower

» *Best bets for nesting birds:* chickadee box, hanging plant basket for House Finches, nest shelf for robins, House Finches and Mourning Dove

» ***Possible hurdles:*** squirrels, clean up, Rock Pigeons, European Starlings

This can be a rewarding, yet challenging, habitat. If trees are far from the apartment building you may not have a problem with squirrels, but even if you are that lucky you still have to deal with pigeons and blackbirds.

Weight-sensitive feeders work well to combat squirrels and pigeons while still allowing cardinals, chickadees and finches. Usually hulled feed such as sunflower hearts and peanuts work well because it won't make a mess under your apartment. If your neighbor doesn't mind, or if you are a cleaning freak like my sister Monica, you might be able to get away with feeding seeds in the shell to avoid the starlings. If that is not possible, then look into getting a caged feeder with a wide cage so starlings and other blackbirds can't cling to the side and stick their heads in to get at the feeding tubes. You can also try upside down suet feeders to keep out starlings and of course finch feeders work well since the feeding ports are too small for larger birds to take over.

If there isn't a water source nearby, consider adding a birdbath to your deck to increase the variety of birds that will come. On the plus side, a birdbath will not make as much of a mess as a bird feeder.

Case #3

New development in the suburbs

» ***Habitat nearby:*** few to no trees with farm fields nearby

» ***Possible birds:*** Black-capped Chickadee, Carolina Chickadee, Mourning Dove, House Finch, American Goldfinch, Dark-eyed Junco, Mallard, Ring-necked Pheasant, American Robin, Tree Swallow, Barn Swallow, Rock Pigeon, Northern Flicker, Eastern Blue-

A new housing addition

bird, Indigo Bunting, Ruby-throated Hummingbird, White-throated Sparrow, Song Sparrow, Wild Turkey, Red-winged Blackbird, American Crow, Canada Goose, Common Grackle, House Sparrow, European Starling, Cooper's Hawk, Red-tailed Hawk, Sharp-shinned Hawk, American Kestrel.

» **Best bets for feeder types:** finch feeders, tray feeders, mealworm feeders, nectar feeders, sunflower or all-purpose feeders

» **Best bets for foods to offer:** Nyjer, sunflower mixes, safflower, cracked and whole corn, fruit mixes, mealworms, nectar, white millet

» **Best bets for nesting birds:** bluebird nest boxes, chickadee nest boxes, nesting platforms for robins, phoebes, swallows, Mourning Doves and House Finches, kestrel box, Purple Martin house

» **Possible hurdles:** slow to attract birds, deer, raptors, raccoons

The upside is that with few or no trees you won't have as big a problem with squirrels and raccoons. (Please note that I wrote "as big a problem." Never underestimate the adaptability of a squirrel or raccoon.) However, a lack of trees also means a lack of cover for birds, so you might want to consider planting some bushes or building a brush pile to offer somewhere for birds to duck into when hawks are flying around.

Another upside to habitat like this is that you have an excellent chance of attracting some of America's most wanted birds like Eastern Bluebirds and Purple Martins. I would still put baffles on the poles for these houses just in case a raccoon decides to make a long trip and raid the houses one night.

If water isn't nearby, adding a birdbath or better yet, installing a small pond will be a great asset for the birds in the area and you will notice a big jump in the birds visiting your yards.

Case #4

Condo complex with feeding allowed only in central area

» **Habitat nearby:** some woods and water like a creek or pond nearby

» **Possible birds:** Northern Cardinal, Black-capped Chickadee, Carolina Chickadee, Mourning Dove, House Finch, American Goldfinch, Dark-eyed Junco, Mallard, Red-breasted Nuthatch, White-breasted Nuthatch, Baltimore Oriole, American Robin, House Wren, Carolina Wren, Tree Swallow, Barn Swallow, Downy Woodpecker, Hairy Woodpecker, Red-bellied Woodpecker, Northern Flicker, Indigo Bunting, Rose-breasted Grosbeak, Ruby-throated Hummingbird, White-throated Sparrow, Song

Sparrow, Red-winged Blackbird, American Crow, Canada Goose, Common Grackle, Blue Jay, House Sparrow, European Starling, Cooper's Hawk, American Kestrel.

A communal outdoor living space

» *Best bets for feeder types:* finch tube feeder, weight-sensitive sunflower or all-purpose feeders, well protected or baffled suet feeders, mealworm feeder, hummingbird feeder, oriole feeder, tray feeder, mealworm feeder, oriole feeder

» *Best bets for foods to offer:* Nyjer, sunflower mixes, safflower, suet, peanuts, mealworms, nectar, grape jelly, fruit, cracked and whole corn, a little white millet

» *Best bets for nesting birds:* chickadee box, wren box, Wood Duck box, nest shelf for robins, phoebes and Mourning Doves, hanging plant baskets for House Finches

» *Possible hurdles:* raccoons, squirrels, deer, clean-up

If the condo association won't allow you to feed birds from your own condo, this solution could be a good compromise: you could offer to set up an area in the commons of your complex. As it may end up being your responsibility to maintain the feeders, it will also be your responsibility to make sure the area stays clean.

A birdbath or a small pond installation can make an attractive and welcome addition for the bird habitat and offering water increases the variety of birds that visit.

Usually in these types of areas, raccoons are already a problem, getting into the garbage. You will need to make sure that the feeding station and any bird houses that are up are well protected against these predators.

Case #5

Small urban lot with trees

» **Habitat nearby:** some trees, but no nearby water

» **Possible birds:** Northern Cardinal, Black-capped Chickadee, Carolina Chickadee, Mourning Dove, House Finch, American Goldfinch, Dark-eyed Junco, Red-breasted Nuthatch, White-breasted Nuthatch, American Robin, House Wren, Caroline Wren, Rock Pigeon, Downy Woodpecker, Hairy Woodpecker, Red-bellied Woodpecker, Northern Flicker, Indigo Bunting, Rose-breasted Grosbeak, Ruby-throated Hummingbird, White-throated Sparrow, American Crow, Canada Goose, Common Grackle, Blue Jay, House Sparrow, European Starling, Cooper's Hawk, American Kestrel.

» **Best bets for feeder types:** finch tube feeder, weight-sensitive sunflower or all-purpose feeders, well protected or baffled suet feeders, upside down finch feeder and suet feeder, mealworm feeder, hummingbird feeder, window feeder

» **Best bets for foods to offer:** Nyjer, sunflower mixes, safflower, suet, peanuts, mealworms, nectar, grape jelly, fruit, cracked and whole corn

» **Best bets for nesting birds:** chickadee box, hanging plant basket for House Finches, nest shelf for robins, House Finches and Mourning Doves, wren box

» **Possible hurdles:** squirrels, raccoons, blackbirds

This is good habitat for attracting birds, but you do need to be ready for squirrels and raccoons. Take special note of how wide open your yard is. You will want to make sure that you can mount feeders on a pole, but not near any lawn furniture, trees or fences so that critters can jump to them. If your yard is too closed in, then weight-sensitive feeders are a must.

A suburban backyard

Keep in mind that, during migration, grackles will be out in force and you will probably have starlings year-round. Hard-shelled seeds such as black oilers and safflower will keep starlings at bay and just plain safflower will give the old heave-ho to the grackles.

If there is not a natural water source nearby, a birdbath will be welcomed by your neighborhood birds. Just remember not to place it too close to the feeder, or squirrels will use it as a launching pad.

Quick-reference checklist

○ What kind of housing do I live in?

○ Based on the kind of habitat that is around me, what kinds of birds am I most likely to attract?

○ If I can't put up feeders, or don't want to, what other options do I have?

○ If I can put up feeders, where will I enjoy seeing them?

○ Based on that, is there an open space in that area for a pole-mounted feeder? (Is it a space away from major yard traffic and far enough away or close enough to windows to prevent window strikes?)

○ If there is not such a space, can I hang feeders from trees, deck-mount or window-mount one in a place where I can enjoy it?

○ What kind of feeder do I want to try, and what is an appropriate food to put in it?

○ How easy is the feeder to clean?

○ After this, experiment to your heart's content. Try different styles of feeders, different foods or try adding a birdbath or other water. If the idea appeals to you, try a nest box or plant some bushes or flowers for the birds. The sky's the limit!

CHAPTER THIRTEEN

Beyond Bird Feeding (I've discovered I'm a bird nut. Now what?)

This book is more of a starter book, to get you interested and hooked on birds. That's right, I'm a bird pusher. So, maybe you've been trying this bird feeding thing and you discovered that you liked it. Where can you go from here? First thing, let me warn you about some of the birders you might meet. Some will tell you that there is only one way to enjoy birds, only one type of field guide that is acceptable and only one binocular that you should use. Those birders are well meaning but incorrect. There are oodles of field guides to choose from, tons of ways to enjoy birds, and new and fantastic binoculars at all price levels developed all the time! You can enjoy birds any way you want to. Here is my manifesto:

There's no right or wrong way to do it, and as long as you aren't harming the birds by the way you enjoy them, do what feels good to you.

OPPOSITE: Bohemian Waxwing

If you enjoy listing and categorizing every bird you see, that's terrific. If you like to peek out your window and see a cardinal at your feeder, that's great. If you think that Red-tailed Hawk flying overhead is your spirit guide, more power to you. Just get out there and watch the birds.

Field Guides

It never hurts to have more than one bird book.

Not every bird that could show up in your yard is in this book. You need a field guide to help you identify birds showing up in the backyard. There are several styles, such as field guides based on the state you live in, some divided by the region you live in the United States or some that include birds from all over the country. Some are photographic and some are illustrated. I've gotten into arguments with people over which is better: photographic versus illustrated. When I started, I preferred the photographic guides because they were easier for me to follow. Now I have both photographic and illustrated. Sometimes a bird will look weird enough you might need two or three field guides to help you identify it.

There's no need to go hog wild and purchase six field guides at once. I recommend starting out with a state or regional field guide to learn the basics and should you ever feel the need for a bigger field guide, get one when you are ready. Starting out with a giant field guide with every bird in the United States can be a little overwhelming. If you just want to know your backyard birds, you will have trouble locating them while sifting through all the other species like petrels, boobies and flycatchers.

Take time to look for different field guides that feel good to you. If you are looking for a starting point, here is a list of books that I personally own and recommend to friends:

Stan Tekiela's state bird guides, *Field Guide to Birds* (Eastern or Western) by Donald and Lillian Stokes, *National Geographic Field Guide to North American Birds*, David Sibley's *Field Guide to North American Birds* (also available in eastern and western regions).

Binoculars

Binoculars are a very personal issue. No one binocular is the best binocular for everyone. There are some brands that are very well known and have quality glass, but that still may not make them work for you. My eyes are close together, and for that reason some binoculars do not fit my face, even those considered to be the best on the market.

Several bird specialty stores and camera stores sell binoculars. At birding festivals, several optics companies will have booths and binoculars and spotting scopes on hand for you to try. You can look through the eyepieces to see how they fit your face, if the design feels comfortable in your hands and if the image is clear.

When it comes to binoculars, bigger isn't necessarily better.

The whole world of binoculars can feel overwhelming, especially if people around you appear to know more than you do. Early on in my birding career, my eyes would glaze over whenever there were any articles on optics in bird magazines. Here are some important tips to keep in mind and to be aware of when you are going in to look at optics. Don't rely on the old, "I'll know the right binoculars when I see the price tag and look through them." There are some important factors to consider:

How do you plan to use the binoculars? Do you just want them to watch birds in your backyard? Do you plan on using your binoculars for watching butterflies? If the answer is yes, you will want close focus binoculars—some will go as close as four feet, others only twelve. Are you planning on being a casual birder just out during the day or are you thinking you could get into hardcore birding and be out at dawn or dusk? For that, be sure to get the best low-light binoculars you can afford.

Then there are all the numbers associated with binoculars: 7x35, 8x42, 10x50. What do they mean? The first number is the magnification—how many times closer the bird appears (seven times, eight times or ten times). The second number refers to the diameter of the objective lens in millimeters, so it would be 35mm, 42mm, 50mm. The more millimeters you have, the more light gets into the binocular, the more clearly you can see when it's

To get an idea of how brightly an image will appear, check the binoculars for an equation similar to this one. It means magnification (eight times closer) times objective lens diameter (in millimeters, of the lens at the bottom of the binoculars).

dim at dawn and dusk. This is going to be important to keep in mind.

You may think you want as high a magnification and as many millimeters as money can buy, but this can also make your binoculars bigger and heavier. I have a hereditary hand tremor and when I use ten-power binoculars, the shaking is more accentuated. As in many things in life, bigger is not necessarily better.

The exit pupil measures how much light is transmitted into your eye by the binocular. Knowing the exit pupil can help you narrow your search for binoculars. You can actually see the exit pupil as a little point of light in the eyepiece if you hold the binocular at arm's length. There's an important equation that determines exit pupil that requires a little bit of math, but you need to pay attention to this part. Don't act like your eyes weren't about to glaze over, because this is the part where my eyes would glaze over before I delved into the wonderful world of binoculars. The magnification and the diameter of the objective lens determines the size of the exit pupil. The equation is to divide the diameter in millimeters by the magnification of the binoculars. So for a 7x35 binocular you would divide 35 by 7 which equals a 5mm exit pupil.

In bright conditions your pupil is between 2mm to 3mm; at dusk and dawn the pupil can be 4mm to 5mm. Most binoculars will bring in more light to your eye than you need, but an ideal exit pupil for birders is usually 4mm or above. So some of the most popular binocular sizes have an exit pupil of 5–5.25 mm.

7x35=5 mm exit pupil

8x42=5.25 mm exit pupil

10x50=5 mm exit pupil

Another important factor in binoculars is waterproofing and warranties. How tough are you on optics? Purchase a pair that is waterproof and has a good warranty. You might be saying to yourself that they will only be on the kitchen table for you to grab easily and watch birds at the feeder, but you never know when they might be knocked off or taken outside for a really exciting bird.

Digiscoping

This is the latest craze hitting the birding world. Basically, digiscoping is using a digital camera with binoculars or a spotting scope to take up close shots of the birds. You can go simple with a point and shoot pocket digital camera or hardcore with a digital SLR camera. The type of camera and the type of scope that you use can affect the quality of your photos.

Digiscoping can be handy if you would like to document a rare bird in the yard or get a souvenir shot of the day an indigo bunting graced your finch feeder. You can try to just hold your camera up to the scope or binocular, but your grip will be shaky and the chances are the photo will be blurry. The technique works best with a spotting scope and if you can find a way to stabilize the camera to the scope. Many optics manufacturers embrace the popularity of this hobby and keep a list of which digital cameras work best with their equipment and even make adaptors to hold the camera steady to your scope. Keep in mind that new digital camera models come out about every six months. The quality of spotting scope you use will greatly affect the quality of the photos that come out.

You can take this a step further with your backyard birding. Some people will go so far as to arrange feeders so that the birds are always feeding at a

Some point and shoot digital cameras with a three to four power zoom can be attached to spotting scopes to get photos of birds. This is called digiscoping.

You can get great photos of birds like this Rose-breasted Grosbeak by digiscoping.

You can also use a Digital SLR camera for digiscoping.

point where you can watch them. You can even go a step further by lacing sticks or decorative vines near the feeder for birds to perch on before they fly in and you a beautiful background for a photo. Before you know it, you will have a ton of digital images to use as greeting cards, calendars, and craft projects.

Connecting With Other Birders

Listservs

Once you are started into the world of birding, you might want to find a way to connect with more of our kind. One of the best ways is to join a listserv for your state. A listerv is an email group that you can subscribe to. You enter your email address to join and any message posted to the list will come to your email address, too. Many of the lists are managed to avoid spam, but depending on the list you can get anywhere from two to fifty messages a day. At times it can be quite exciting, especially during spring migration as people start to report when they see species such as Rose-breasted Grosbeaks and Baltimore Orioles so you can know when to anticipate them in your yard. If an unusual bird is reported near where you live you can find out about it and maybe go see it. One day, I learned from a Minnesota listserv that a Snowy Owl was seen seven blocks from where I live.

You might find birding companions this way, too. I met some of my favorite companions through birding listservs. Many people will offer to carpool to remote areas or announce bird club field trip offerings. To find out what listservs are in your state, use a search engine like www.google.com and type in the name of your state and the words "bird" and "listserv" or try the name of your state with the words "bird" and "email list."

Bird Festivals

Bird festivals are held all over the country. Chances are there could be at least one organized in your home state. These are usually weekends of well-organized birding trips and lectures. They often happen when there are peak chances for seeing special species. A few examples that come to mind are the Rivers and Wildlife Celebration that happens in mid-March in Nebraska to celebrate the spring migration and watch thousands of Sandhill Cranes along the Platte River; the Rio Grande Valley Bird Festival that happens in early November where you can see Texas and Mexican specialties like Green Jays, Crested Caracaras and Great Kiskadees; or the Detroit Lakes Festival of Birds in Minnesota that happens in late May when you can see great spring warblers like Black-burnian Warbler or Northern Parula, or shorebirds like Marbled Godwits and Wilson's Phalaropes.

Blackburnian Warbler

What's ideal about bird festivals is that they are organized for people who have never visited the area to show you the great spots to see certain species so that you can bird there again on your own in the future. Some festivals are so fun that many people return year after year for the birds as well as the camaraderie. Personally, I have met some wonderful friends from around the country who I only see at birding festivals and it is an added dimension of fun to reconnect with them. Another advantage is that I know if I'm in southern California, I have a friend to call on when I visit and she can show me the great birds where she lives and I am happy to reciprocate if she ever comes to Minnesota.

Local Bird Clubs

There can be all different kinds of bird clubs in your state, usually easily found through searching on the internet. There are Audubon chapters, ornithologists' societies (which are usually made up of birders rather than ornithologists) or general bird clubs. Clubs usually offer members field trips, interesting guest speakers or fun newsletters and magazines about birds in your area. Stop into your local bird specialty store and see if they have contact information for bird clubs in your area.

National Birding Organizations

American Birding Association
www.americanbirding.org
P.O. Box 6599
Colorado Springs, CO 80934-6599

This national birding association offers great publications, conventions, workshops and birding tours. There's also the opportunity to get involved in a number of exciting and worthwhile conservation and education programs.

Cornell Lab of Ornithology
www.birds.cornell.edu
159 Sapsucker Woods Road
Ithaca, NY 14850

The Cornell Lab is a nonprofit membership institution whose mission is to interpret and conserve the earth's biological diversity through research, education and citizen science focused on birds. Member benefits include subscriptions to Cornell publications and the opportunity to participate in Citizen Science projects such as Project Feeder Watch. I've participated in their Golden-winged Warbler Atlas Project and a friend and I drove around searching for Golden-winged Warblers and documenting where they can be found in Minnesota. Heck, I even got the opportunity to go look for the Ivory-billed Woodpecker through Cornell. It's a great membership.

Resources

Bird Feeder Companies

Aspects, Inc.
www.aspectsinc.com
P.O. Box 408
245 Child Street
Warren, RI 02885
1-888-ASPECTS

Birds Choice
www.birdschoice.com
477 Vogt Lane
Chilton, WI 53014
1-800-817-8833

Brome Bird Care (makers of the
Squirrel Buster Deluxe)
www.bromebirdcare.com
331 Knowlton Road
Knowlton, Quebec
Canada
J0E 1V0
1-800-856-5685

Droll Yankees
www.drollyankees.com
27 Mill Road
Foster, RI 02825
1-800-352-9164 or 860-779-8980

Duncraft
www.duncraft.com
102 Fisherville Road
Concord, NH 03303
1-888-879-5095

Heritage Farms
www.heritagefarms.biz
1462 U.S. Route 20 Bypass
Cherry Valley, IL 61016
1-800-845-2473

Perky-Pet Products Co.
www.perky-pet.com
2201 South Wabash Street
Denver, CO 80231
303-751-9000

Woodlink
www.woodlink.net
1500 Woodlink Drive
P.O. Box 508
Mount Ayr, IA 50854

Bird-Related Magazines

Birds and Blooms
www.birdsandblooms.com
Reiman Publications
5400 South 60th Street
Greendale, WI 53129

Bird Watcher's Digest
http://birdwatchersdigest.com
149 Acme Street
P.O. Box 110
Marietta, OH 45750

Birder's World
www.birdersworld.com
Kalmbach Publishing Co.
21027 Crossroads Circle
P.O. Box 1612
Waukesha, WI 53187-1612

WildBird Magazine
www.wildbirdmagazine.com
P.O. Box 57900
Los Angeles, CA 90057

National Chains of Wild Bird Specialty Stores

Wild Birds Unlimited, Inc.
www.wbu.com

Wild Bird Center
www.wildbirdcenter.com

Index